WOMAN BE WHOLE

by

Jacqueline T. Flowers

Llumina
Christian
Books

Unless otherwise indicated, all scripture quotations
are from the King James Version of the Bible.

Fourth Printing 2000

© 2011 Jacqueline T. Flowers
© 1992

ISBN: 978-1-62550-393-0

Printed in the United States of America by Llumina Christian Books

TABLE OF CONTENTS

DEDICATION

First, "WOMAN BE WHOLE" is written for the glory and honor of our Heavenly Father for His great love for us and His abundant blessings.

Second, to my husband for loving me as Christ loves the church and for his patience, understanding and support as I yield to the perfect will of God.

Third, to our children Demetrius, Tiana, and Jerry, Jr., because they are certainly among the generation of the mighty and descendants of the most High God on this earth.

"WOMAN BE WHOLE" is also dedicated to my mother, the late Betty L. Jackson, and my stepfather, the late Doris Jackson for their encouragement and prayers.

i

INTRODUCTION

As a young child, I never realized my life would take the course it took. Reflecting back, as many of you will as you read this book, there were so many devastating experiences. Many of the circumstances I experienced could have destroyed me. Yet there is one truth which I live by to this very day, that brought me out of torment and emotional pain, to a life of peace and absolute victory. It is not what happens to us in life but rather our attitude that determines the end result. By making this statement I do not mean to imply that my life is challenge free; challenges still arise. I simply see them as opportunities for growth and development. As a result, victory once attained, brings lasting reward.

The decision to live by this truth, which I will reveal throughout the pages of this book, ultimately fashioned my destiny. I was not responsible for many of the events that transpired in my life; however, the effects were brutal and lasting. In most instances, as were many of you, I was a victim of what seemed to be an endless nightmare. In other circumstances, I experienced devastating consequences because of unwise decisions I made at crucial times in my life. No matter how the situation began, you can experience (even as I have) a new life with new aspirations, self worth, and total completeness as a woman, if you are willing to take this "JOURNEY TO WHOLENESS."

If you will follow the principles outlined on the pages of this book intently, and discipline yourself to apply them, you will rise to a dimension of living that brings endless peace and joy.

You, too, can become a woman experiencing wholeness no matter what tragedies you have experienced in the past. I have talked to women who have been molested, raped, abused (verbally, emotionally, and physically), battered, divorced, involved in adulterous relationships, or their mate was involved in adultery. There have been women who have gone to churches hurting, only to be approached by the Pastor for sex. And, as a result, have never gone back to any church. Women are hurting, but the hurt can cease. The healing is progressive and begins with a quality decision to overcome. As you read this book you will be provoked as never before to make some quality decisions. Life is filled with choices, and the choices selected will establish the course of future events and relationships for success or failure; victory or defeat.

The truths outlined throughout the pages of this book, have literally taken a bruised, battered, emotionally shattered and devastated life, and transformed it into one filled with purpose, power, peace, total wholeness and God's richest blessings in abundance. Will you be one to discover your vast potential and unlimited resources? You have been fashioned for "God's Glory" and nothing can stop you from being totally unique and destined for greatness. So, let's begin "your" JOURNEY TO WHOLENESS.

CHAPTER ONE

FORGETTING THE PAST

Perhaps one of the most difficult tasks for every woman is to discard the hurts and frustrations of the past (never ruled by feelings or opinions of others or negative emotions). This is probably largely attributed to our make-up. We value precious memories and are affectionately sentimental about the special things of life. On the other hand, we are tender-hearted and more emotional than men. Our emotions can be adversely affected in a greater measure than the average man when facing abuse and conflict.

All too often, when heartache is experienced we can recall in a most vivid manner the intricate details surrounding its happening. Daily we may find ourselves rehearsing the grim horrors of the past, never really breaking free of the haunting effects, never progressing onward, but constantly detained by yesterday's mishaps.

I was born the fourth child in a family of six (four boys and two girls). My first and most traumatic encounter with heartache and mental torment came when I was four years of age. Little did I realize I would experience an ordeal that would torment and emotionally cripple me throughout childhood, adolescence, and even into the early years of womanhood.

My mother was at work that evening when my father entered my room. He removed me from my bed, never saying a word, and took me to the room he and my mother shared. The fact that I was his own biological daughter mattered not, for it was there that he molested me. This experience permanently scarred the imprint in my mind of a father and a father's love. Not only was my view distorted concerning my father, it was distorted concerning who I was. I didn't really understand the gravity of what had taken place, neither was I responsible for this shameful act. I only knew I felt ugly, dirty, afraid, and hurt. With this aching in my mind and body, somehow I knew I could never breathe a word of what happened to my mother, or to anyone. This was the epitome of horrors and the beginning of my nightmares.

The total impact this experience would have on my life was not completely realized; yet inwardly, there was something missing. I felt I was not as good as the other children I associated with. There was a feeling of inferiority, a feeling of lostness. The awareness that I had been violated in the worst manner was not clear to me at this point. This man, who totally devastated my life, had been my idol, my daddy.

The father-daughter relationship was over and I would never again trust him. Never again would I sit upon his lap, hugging his neck with the expectation of protection, love, and security. Even in my young child's mind, there was this realization that what he had done to me was not motivated by love. A whirlwind began within me, for I had no hope of ever truly knowing or experiencing the genuine love of a father.

How could I ever forget? Would I forget? How could I overcome the feelings of uncleanliness? How could I ever play with my little friends and not feel inferior to them? When would the pain and memories cease to torment me? When would the effects of this nightmare, kept secret in the dark crevice of my mind, end? I dared not tell a soul and until the writing of this book, my secret remained concealed within me.

It was not very long after this ordeal that late one evening while my parents were at work, a man which I identified as our neighbor, entered our home. My three older brothers and I were asleep. Again, I was taken from my room and raped.

I remember rehearsing the story over and over before the police officer as he arrested our neighbor, who swore he would get me for this. With all that I was feeling inside, everything was so foggy. My father told the policeman that our neighbor broke into our home while he and my mother were at work. How

I wished the officer had taken the man I no longer saw as my daddy, for something within me detested his presence. He had caused me pain too; he caused me torment.

I was so young and the details concerning the rape were foggy in my mind. Was it possible that I had accused the wrong man? Was the man actually my daddy and not our neighbor. Some days later I heard our neighbor had been released and all charges against him dismissed. Fear gripped me and terror paralyzed me emotionally.

We moved to another place of residence and shortly afterwards my parents divorced. In an effort to drown the memories of these ordeals I never addressed my father as daddy again. I refused any form of communication with him. My mother never talked against him, nor did she force me to establish a relationship with him. I remained distant from him until his death.

Years passed and as I approached adolescence with so many memories haunting me, there was this hunger for love, this need to be accepted, the need to belong. I tried to be impressionable in order to have friends. At the age of fourteen, I was teased and taunted by my peers about being a virgin. They knew nothing of my past. I was not interested in sex or young men. Yet, I desperately wanted acceptance. I tried to compromise and nine months later I had a five pound, thirteen and one half ounce baby boy. Today, he is a graduate of Prairie View A & M University, with a Bachelor's in Engineering. That one isolated experience of compromise did not rid me of feelings of insecurity, loneliness, worthlessness, inferiority, and a fear of rejection. As a matter of truth, my compromise compounded my fears.

At the age of fourteen my life took a drastic turn. It was during this time that I was told about the Lord Jesus Christ, received Him as Savior of my life, and experienced water baptism. I was told that now I was a child of God, a new creature; yet I did not feel new. No one was familiar with the horror of what I experienced as a young child, or the failures encountered as I entered my teenage years. Even though I was what was called a "new creature", a Christian, the pain was still there, the hurt within had not gone. The feelings of being ugly, unclean, and rejected were still very much a part of me.

What could I do to rid myself of these feelings? How could I escape this whirlwind? Could being a Christian make the difference? I did not realize the answer was soon to come.

I attended church regularly, loving the Lord Jesus Christ with all my heart. There were still many flaws in my "Christian Character" and my "Christian Witness" as I continued my search for acceptance. The reality of God accepting me into His family was not really clear. The effects of my past remained very prevalent in my mind and served as the ruling factor in every facet of my life. Consequently, the circumstances of the past affected my attitude about life, people, and so much more.

In my senior year of high school, I entered a marital relationship which had no basis other than a lot of mixed emotions, misconceptions, and false security. Somehow, in my mind, I rationalized that this marriage would erase my past and give me a sense of worth, a sense of wholeness and completeness. I felt I would experience a sense of belonging, a sense of acceptance. On the contrary, I was about to experience another ordeal that would be added to my diary of horrors. In the frame of mind I was in and the condition of my emotions, marriage was the last thing I needed. There was absolutely no foundation to build upon.

As an eighteen year old, in my senior year of high school, marrying a twenty-five year old, I had much to learn about life, people, and this God I so desperately loved and longed to know. It was in this marital relationship that I experienced verbal and physical abuse that I had never imagined possible. It was not clear to me which was worse, the harsh vulgar words which scarred me for years, the threats of being stabbed to death, or the actual blows against my face. This man was doing to me the exact same things I observed my biological father do to my mother.

He said he never really wanted me. I was the result of a bet he made with his friends. He blatantly said, "I told them since they could not get you, I would." It was during this time I discovered he was involved in an adulterous relationship with a woman I befriended. She visited our home on a number of occasions and I extended her kindness never realizing she was sleeping with the man I married. As a young Christian I was bewildered. The woman I befriended was the church musician, my sister in the Lord. How could this be? Was this the behavior I would find among those who professed to live as the Christ I read about in the Bible? I turned cold inside. There was a desire to be loved, yet a deep distrust of all men. I worked at a convalescent center after graduating from high school. My husband, at that time, never kept a job long enough for us to move ahead financially.

Throughout the course of this situation, what little self-worth I may have possessed, if any, slowly diminished. I can recall an occasion when the situation was so horrid, that I cashed my check at the end of a pay period, placed the money in my shoes and literally walked on it during an eight hour shift. I had no place to hide my money and if I turned it over to my husband, it would have been wasted on drugs and only God knows what else. My feet were in excruciating pain, but at least even this was bearable after all that was staring me in the face. Then I had my second child, a daughter.

I had not really gotten to know this man before marriage. The drugs and women had been concealed. One incident led to another. I was so naive and gullible as a young Christian. After several nights, weeks, months of depression, discouragement and tormenting threats of abuse, the marriage terminated in divorce and I felt responsible for the failure of this union. Leaving the situation behind, I carried the memories, past mistakes, my son and daughter with me to begin a new life. I attended college at the University of Houston at night and worked an eight hour job during the day. I traveled by bus working and attending school. My life seemed to be a direct reflection of my mother's. I remember watching my biological father beat her viciously until she divorced him. She was then forced to provide for six of us, working irregular hours just to provide for us. Our clothes were purchased from Goodwill Stores and as a means of support, the State provided powdered milk, cheese, powdered eggs, spam, and beans. I was determined to rise above my circumstances. Mother never begged, neither would I. Living in an apartment, with two children, attending college, and working an eight hour job required much. I soon dropped out of college and began to work feverishly to gain some ground financially.

My children were innocent and even though I had come into the knowledge of the Lord Jesus Christ, I did not know how to overcome the challenges of life. I experienced challenge after challenge and made mistake after mistake while searching for wholeness, while searching to be a complete person. Sure, I looked complete on the outside, but inwardly I was a miserable wreck. There seemed to be a force of evil that had set the stage to destroy me. Could I ever become a complete person? Could I, now a single parent, actually raise my son and my daughter successfully? Could I forget the past and its horrid effects? Would past failures and past mistakes, cling to me forever? I lost confidence in myself and in others.

In the church, the one place I hoped to find peace, I met Pastors with beautiful wives and children who made advances toward me. What was wrong with me? What was happening? I needed answers to my questions; solutions to my problems. The last thing I wanted was to be "the other woman" or party to destroying someone else's life, when my own life was in shambles. I detested the flirty insinuations, and I lost confidence in many who professed to be men of God. In the back of my mind I questioned the integrity and character of every person declaring himself to be a man of God. I never succumbed to lust filled invitations. As a matter of truth, I felt growing up in a traditional Baptist church was a joke, to say the least.

Often I wondered if life was really worth it. It seemed that suicide would end it all. I believe God kept me with these words:

Psalm 139:7-13

Whither shall I go from thy spirit? Or whither shall I flee from thy presence? If I ascend up into heaven, thou art there: if I make my bed in hell, behold, thou art there. If I take the wings of the morning, and dwell in the uttermost parts of the sea; even there shall thy hand lead me, and thy right hand shall hold me. If I say, surely the darkness shall cover me; even the night shall be light about me. Yea, the darkness hideth not from thee; but the night shineth as the day: the darkness and the light are both alike to thee. For thou hast possessed my reins: thou hast covered me in my mother's womb.

God kept me at times when I could not keep myself. I am persuaded that He placed deep within me a yearning to rise out of this state of hopelessness and despair to a new beginning. I was not aware then, as I am now, that the Holy Spirit led me to the following scripture and established my life by it:

Philippians 3:10-14

"That I may know him, and the power of his resurrection, and the fellowship of his sufferings, being made conformable unto his death; if by any means I might attain unto the resurrection of the dead. Not as though I had already attained, either were already perfect: but I follow after, if that I may apprehend that for which also I am apprehended of Christ Jesus. Brethren, I count not myself to have apprehended: but this one thing I do, forgetting those things which are behind, and

reaching forth unto those things which are
before, I press toward the mark for the prize
of the high calling of God in Christ Jesus."

The words from these verses contained the components that established my destiny. What refreshing words! I did not have to accept life in light of my past as being my lot in life; however, I could rise to a new dimension in life. After reading this scripture I could have chosen to drown myself in self-pity, or drown myself with hate, anger, unforgiveness, bitterness and resentment for all that had happened in my life. What would I benefit? It was at this point that I decided even though I did not understand why I experienced all that transpired in my life, I would not allow my past to govern how I would live life on planet earth for the days to come. No longer would I allow guilt, shame, hurt, anger, resentment, unforgiveness or bitterness to dictate how I would treat others who were not responsible for what I had experienced. My experiences would not be a tombstone but a steppingstone to true freedom.

In **Philippians 3:10-14,** the Apostle Paul talks about becoming acquainted with the Lord Jesus Christ and understanding all that Jesus accomplished for mankind through the power of His resurrection. Paul expresses the desire to know Christ and His association with suffering. These verses reveal how a man can be made conformable unto the death of Christ as he experiences the death of the old nature (old thought patterns and behavioral trends) and come to know the way of righteousness as a new creature. (This process is explained in greater detail in the following chapters).

Paul further elaborates on his imperfections and inability to understand all things--but his commitment to do this one significant thing, "forgetting those things which are behind and reaching forth unto those things which are before, I press toward the mark for the prize of the high calling of God in Christ Jesus." No person has the capacity to mentally deny the transpiration of certain events in life. We cannot extract from our minds the ugly details of past experiences, but every person can make a willful, conscious decision not to allow events of the past to influence their future. This is exactly what I did. I made the decision to force myself to live everyday free from the influence of the past. I decided to exercise the power of my will to live in every word I read in the Bible. To forget simply means to refuse to allow the events of the past to govern one's future in a negative manner. We don't have to be adversely ruled by the mishaps of yesterday.

There was so much more life had to offer and I was determined to break free of the chains that enslaved me. Nothing that happened in my past would govern future relationships, future aspirations, future desires and dreams. I could not deny that I had been a victim of rape. I could not deny that I had been molested. I could not deny I had been battered, and verbally abused on several occasions, just as I could not deny that I made some extremely unwise decisions for which I suffered the consequences. These were the facts, but God's Word revealed something greater than the facts. In spite of the negatives, I decided that the experiences of my past would not hold me back and rob me of the joy of living, the joy of being a complete woman, the joy of being whole. It was with this information that I forged ahead. Decisions were facing me. I could succumb to the influence of the past or I could decide to rise out of the emotional pit that held me hostage for years. The decision to not be a failure prevailed, as God's word was unfolded before me.

Isaiah 43:15-21

I am the Lord, your Holy One, the Creator of Israel, your King. Thus saith the Lord, which maketh a way in the sea, and a path in the mighty waters; Which bringeth forth the chariot and horse, the army and the power; they shall lie down together, they shall not rise: they are extinct, they are quenched as tow. Remember ye not the former things, neither consider the things of old. Behold, I will do a new thing; now it shall spring forth;

*shall ye not know it? I will even make a way in
the wilderness, and rivers in the desert. The beast
of the field shall honour me, the dragons and the
owls: because I give waters in the wilderness, and
rivers in the desert, to give drink to my people,
my chosen. This people have I formed for myself;
they shall shew forth my praise.*

God had formed me for Himself and chosen me to exemplify
His power and His goodness in the earth. Boy!!! Was I ever
ready for something fresh, something new to begin in my life.
I was tired of the wilderness I had been living in; a wilderness
mentality, a desert lifestyle and the drunkenness on the torment
of failure. The need to drink of God's power and the freshness
of life gave me the motivation for change. This need for change
outweighed the urge to remain in what I call a dungeon of torment
and a prison filled with endless nightmares. Hope was restored
and this hope stabilized me. It was an anchor for my soul, because
prior to this time I had no hope, but now I had something that was
secure--THE WORD OF GOD.

Hebrews 6:18-19
*That by two immutable things, in which it was
impossible for God to lie, we might have a
strong consolation, who have fled for refuge to
lay hold upon the hope set before us: Which
hope we have as an anchor of the soul, both
sure and stedfast, and which entereth into that
within the veil;...*

Romans 15:4
*For whatsoever things were written aforetime,
were written for our learning, that we through
patience and comfort of the scriptures might
have hope.*

CHAPTER TWO

A NEW BEGINNING
(FROM BONDAGE TO FREEDOM)

How could a woman so brutally battered, broken, and bewildered experience wholeness? Was it really possible for me to be a total human being?

In July of the year 1984, the Lord spoke these words to my heart so clearly and more distinguishably than I had ever known, "You are greatly loved and chosen to share the truth of My Word with many." In astonishment I made my argument known. How could an Almighty God choose a divorced woman with shattered emotions, brutal memories and decayed hopes and dreams? I asked, "Lord would you choose me after all the mistakes I have made, all the failures I have experienced, all the bad decisions? Surely I am not fit to tell anybody anything about You or Your Word. Besides, I have always been taught that You do not use women in the capacity of ministering Your Word." I limited God to my experiences. I failed to realize He knew all and was greater than anything I could have experienced in life. His Word came back to me like fire. "I will prove you before all men, because I have chosen you." God further impressed upon my heart, " You are amazed at what I have called others to do, behold, I have called you to do even greater."

I was chosen by God! I could not deny this, for every fiber of my being sensed His love and compassion. This experience set me on the path to recovery. What was ahead was uncertain in my mind. I only knew I heard the voice of God and this caused me to search the scriptures as never before. I needed proper insight, illumination in order to experience the proper changes. The foundation for change had to be the Word of God. I was certain of this. I had received the Lord Jesus Christ into my heart as Savior, yet, somehow I knew something was missing. On the outside I appeared to be a complete woman, confident and secure. Yet, inwardly I was in bondage; held hostage by my own emotions.

In spite of these feelings of inadequacy I trusted God's word to heal me. If God would prove me before all men, surely He would effect a work on the inside of me that would prepare me for what He predestined me to do. It was evident I did not possess the total understanding of how this healing would consummate. I only knew it was vital if I was to be successful at fulfilling God's plan. This inward work was also essential before I could totally enjoy the benefits of marriage. It would be difficult, to say the least, for me to love any man until I could first love God and then myself. How void of knowledge I was. I longed for family. I wanted a home and a stable environment for my children; yet, I was too emotionally scarred for marriage. There needed to be a total healing, a total emotional and spiritual break from my past before committing to any one else.

In the absence of full knowledge, I asked the Lord to hand pick a husband for me. One who would love me as Christ loves the Church.

Ephesians 5:25
Husbands, love your wives, even as Christ also loved the church, and gave himself for it;....

I felt certain if God brought my husband and if this man would love me as Christ loves the church, the process of inner healing would be expedited. It was God's grace and abundant mercy that kept me at this crucial time because the message still was not clear. I did not realize that the healing process began when I disciplined myself to seek the Lord Jesus with my whole heart. It was not marriage that would bring healing or wholeness, neither would it expedite the healing process.

The emotional trauma I experienced was a result of continued disappointments. Only my relationship with an Almighty God

12

could effect a permanent healing. I use the word "relationship" because mere knowledge of or shallow acquaintance with the Lord Jesus Christ, without a genuine commitment to Him, would prove fruitless. I had to learn to appropriate the Word of God by practical application and continuous yieldedness to truth.

At age twenty-seven (27) I met Jerry Flowers, and after twenty-five years of marriage he still loves me as Christ loves the church. But even in marriage the effects of what was going on inside me had to be dealt with. There was a great work to be accomplished within me. The old had to be completely eradicated and the new firmly established. This would take time, discipline, and consistent effort.

In April 1986, Jerry and I were extremely disenchanted with various ministries and had very little confidence or respect for many professing to be men of God. We knew we needed a pastor and we needed to be submitted in a local church. We could not judge the man God fashioned to be our Pastor by past experiences with others.

Jeremiah 3:15
And I will give you pastors according to mine heart, which shall feed you with knowledge and understanding.

God called pastors to nurture His people in spiritual things; to feed them with knowledge and understanding. Pastors are called to be sensitive to the spiritual needs of the people, hearing with the heart and understanding by the Spirit how to administer the Word of God in a manner that would absolutely transform the lives of those who would commit to hear and apply the principles presented in the Word of God.

My husband and I began to search the scriptures for clarity and found that God's Word is non-negotiable and this truth had to be settled within the heart and be apparent in lifestyle if a man will enjoy God's best.

The truth was unveiled in **Mark 11:25-26**. I knew I would never be the same. There was a desire in my heart that no

materialistic item could compensate for and the revelation from
this passage contained the key.

Mark 11:25-26

*And when ye stand praying, forgive, if ye
have ought against any: that your Father
also which is in heaven may forgive you your
trespasses. But if ye do not forgive, neither
will your Father which is in heaven forgive
your trespasses."*

There is a powerful principle we all must learn from the above
verses that will literally transform our lives. Unless we walk in
forgiveness, we jeopardize our fellowship with God. From these
verses something dawned on me in a fresh illuminating way.
Before I could enjoy God's best, I had to forgive. It became
apparent to me that I had been holding on to the shame and guilt
of my past because I had never totally forgiven significant people
who abused me at a young age, nor had I forgiven myself. Looking
back at all I endured, could I really forgive? "Healing will not
come, wholeness will not come without genuine forgiveness."
It would only take a moment in time for me to forgive. At the
point of genuine forgiveness, satan would no longer have a
right to torment me and rob me of the blessings of God. Upon
hearing these words, I was willing to do whatever it took to be
a complete person and God's Spirit provided the answer. I had
heard from other ministers about the importance of forgiveness,
but no one ever explicitly explained how to forgive. The Spirit of
God ushered me into a place of insight, and I began to walk in the
fullness of this God ordained commandment. Forgiveness was
not my option but rather a requirement if I desired to be totally
free and enjoy the blessings of God.

I simply made the decision to no longer penalize others for
their actions against me, by releasing them in the spirit of love
and choosing as an act of my own will to forgive. All of this
was possible because God's love had been shed in my heart by

the Holy Spirit. I had the capability to love as God loves, not because of, but in spite of. God's power was available to show me how.

Romans 5:1-5

Therefore being justified by faith, we have peace with God through our Lord Jesus Christ: By whom also we have access by faith into this grace wherein we stand, and rejoice in hope of the glory of God. And not only so, but we glory in tribulations also: knowing that tribulation worketh patience; And patience, experience; and experience, hope: And hope maketh not ashamed; because the love of God is shed abroad in our hearts by the Holy Ghost which is given unto us.

The truths in these verses revealed my justification, my innocence. I had a right to stand in the presence of God guiltless. Hope was kindled in me and faith came. God loved me in spite of the past and required that I love others as He loved me. I literally discharged the offense by exercising the power of my will to enter into agreement with God. This simply means I had to condition myself to live in God's Word no matter what I encountered. From that day forward I would treat others as God treats all men, seeing them through His eyes of compassion. My total deliverance became a reality as I released the love of God, the ability of God, and the power of God. I disciplined myself to do what the Word of God said no matter how I felt and no matter what the circumstance.

With this principle I chose to no longer penalize myself for past failures. To live free from any form of oppression would require change and change was a choice--**MY CHOICE!** I had made more mistakes in life than I wanted to remember. I experienced loneliness, rejection and many of the fears those of you reading this book have. I had experienced the sorrow and pain of losing loved ones to tragic deaths and such severe emotional pain until life on this earth seemed almost unbearable. You can't imagine some of the horrible things I witnessed and experienced as a child. Yet, in spite of it all, the healing power of God prevailed. He is not only the God who heals the physical body, He is the God who also heals the emotionally scarred and crippled. You can reap the benefits of this powerful truth as well. **THE CHOICE IS YOURS.**

Deuteronomy 30:19 (Living Bible)
*I call heaven and earth to witness against you that today I have set before you life or death, blessing or curse. Oh, that **YOU WOULD CHOOSE LIFE**; that you and your children might live!*

Luke 10:38-42
*Now it came to pass, as they went, that he (Jesus) entered into a certain village: and a certain woman named Martha received him into her house. And she had a sister called Mary, which also sat at Jesus' feet, and heard his word. But Martha was cumbered about much serving, and came to him, and said, Lord, dost thou not care that my sister hath left me to serve alone? bid her therefore that she help me. And Jesus answered and said unto her, Martha, Martha, thou art careful and troubled about many things: But one thing is needful: and Mary **HATH CHOSEN THAT GOOD PART**, which shall not be taken away from her.*

There could be no bitterness in my heart against those who caused me pain in any fashion. Harboring bitterness would only enhance suffering and close the spiritual channels through which God could pour His mercy (forgiveness) and His grace (unmerited favor) upon me. The ball was in my court. I had the advantage.

Hebrews 12:15
Looking diligently lest any man fail of the grace of God; lest any root of bitterness springing up trouble you, and thereby many be defiled;...

God revealed His forgiveness towards me in the following scriptures:

Psalm 103:1-3
Bless the Lord, O my soul: and all that is within me, bless his holy name. Bless the Lord, O my soul, and forget not all his benefits: Who forgiveth all thine iniquities; who healeth all thy diseases;...

Psalm 103:12-13
As far as the east is from the west, so far hath he removed our transgressions from us. Like as a father pitieth his children, so the Lord pitieth them that fear (reverently respect) him.

Isaiah 43:25 (Amplified)
I, even I am He who blots out and cancels your transgressions for My Own sake and I will not remember your sins.

Isaiah 1:18
Come now, and let us reason together, saith the Lord: though your sins be as scarlet, they shall be as white as snow; though they be red like crimson, they shall be as wool.

God's forgiveness of my sins was a benefit I could enjoy. However, this benefit was contingent upon my willingness to forgive others. I made the choice. I had to dismiss the negative facts, embrace the truth outlined in God's Word, reject the abusive words and purpose in my heart to rise out of the dilemma that plagued my life for years. Even as God totally eradicated my sins against Him, I totally canceled the offense of others by not allowing myself to take offense no matter what their actions.

The truth in God's Word initiated a point of decision. Truth accepted must be visible. To implement the process of change God began within me would take time. All that I was began with a culmination and accumulation of everything that happened in my past, my interpretation of what happened, my belief and acceptance of what happened, how I perceived myself and others, and what I had been speaking. Yes, I was a composite portfolio of every experience. I alone could manage my portfolio.

John 8:30-32

As he spake these words, many believed on him. Then said Jesus to those Jews which believed on him, If ye continue in my word, then are ye my disciples indeed; And ye shall know the truth, and the truth shall make you free.

I wanted to be free. I wanted to be emotionally sound, emotionally whole. My desire was to be balanced in my mind, more particularly in my thoughts. This desire was driving me as never before. Jesus said if I continued in the word, I would be a disciple indeed. A disciple is a disciplined one. I understood this to mean that if I would apply His Word to my life daily, discipline and consistency would bring freedom. Consequently, my freedom would not be instant but progressive; each day would be a shedding process. As God taught me to love and reverence Him, it was imperative that I love myself as the woman He created me to be. I had never truly known self-love. This was a prerequisite before I could freely and genuinely love others. I had to accept myself as one fashioned by God, and the highest level of freedom and self-worth (self-esteem) I could ever experience was in Him. With this knowledge I was able to see myself in totality. Something significantly different was taking place, a metamorphosis, a transformation. The Greek word for transformed is "metamorpho." This is where the word metamorphosis is derived. A metamorphosis is a complete and total change. It is an inward change that establishes external change. Why? Because all growth is dependant upon change. Growth is a steady progression towards full development.

Unlike a caterpillar's metamorphosis, which is a one-time event which changes him completely, the metamorphosis I was undergoing would be an ongoing process. This process of change would continue as long as I lived on planet earth.

Philippians 1:6
Being confident of this very thing, that he which hath begun a good work in you will perform it until the day of Jesus Christ:...

Yes, I could see. I had been declared innocent before God through my acceptance of His Son by faith. I had to rehearse in my mind and visualize God's Word working within me. Therefore, I could not hold a grudge or the effects of an offense against others no matter what the assault. God was working in me for a far greater purpose.

Philippians 2:13 (Amplified)
Not in your own strength for it is God who is all the while effectually at work in you-- energizing and creating in you the power and desire both to will and to work for His good pleasure and satisfaction and delight.

God was and still is working in His people, creating in us the abilty, the energy, and the desire both to will and to work for His good pleasure.

Sure, I had experienced challenges, but now I possessed comprehensive insight. I could see those challenges in a different light and draw wisdom for the future from the experiences of the past. I was a new woman with a new beginning. Others told me I was a new creature when I received Jesus, but I had not heard any one explicitly explain how to overcome a diseased mind. I was a trinity; simply, I was spirit, living in a physical body, having a soul(mind). It was not my body or spirit that was diseased. It was my mind, my emotions, my desires. I never realized the negative words I had been believing about myself, my past, and others held me in bondage.

After making the decision to forgive others and to forgive myself, I began to live in God's Word and speak words that were liberating, words that brought freedom and words that brought deliverance. Those words were already written in black and white for me in "the Bible." The same mouth I used to speak negative, unprofitable words, I began to speak words of life. God's Word came alive in me.

Psalm 45:1b
...my tongue is the pen of a ready writer.

Proverbs 4:20-22
My son, attend to my words; incline thine ear unto my sayings. Let them not depart from thine eyes; keep them in the midst of thine heart. For they are life unto those that find them, and health to all their flesh.

Joshua 1:8
This book of the law shall not depart out of thy mouth; but thou shalt meditate therein day and night, that thou mayest observe to do according to all that is written therein: for then thou shalt make thy way prosperous, and then thou shalt have good success.

Bringing my mind, will, emotions, desires, imagination, behavior and tongue into agreement with God ordered the very course of my life. I began to guard the words that I spoke and control the thoughts of my mind. I searched the scriptures for answers. Controlling my thoughts was important because I had been ruled by the negative thoughts of the past. I was a product of what I had been believing and speaking. My life had been governed by a lie. How I perceived all that happened in my past ruled my life. I did not know how to discern fact from truth. For years the tormenting facts held me in bondage, but when God revealed to me that He did not regard the negative about my life, only truth, I could implement the truth He revealed.

Many of you reading this book believe a lie. You see, if you believe a thing is true, even though it is a lie, it is truth to you. Facts only tell what has happened or is happening. Truth is eternal and tells what really is. Truth brings freedom. The facts in my life revealed my past and present condition, for I allowed circumstances to determine my self-worth.

Proverbs 23:7a
For as he thinketh in his heart, so is he:...

I thought I had no self-worth. I believed I had no self-worth. I spoke as one having no worth. Consequently, this was exemplified in my life. How I saw myself dictated how I lived. Jesus said in **Matthew 6:22-23**, *"The light of the body is the eye: if therefore thine eye be single, thy whole body shall be full of light. But if thine eye be evil, thy whole body shall be full of darkness. If therefore the light that is in thee be darkness, how great is that darkness!"* The eye is the light of the body, referring to how man sees himself, God, others and circumstances. Light refers to understanding, perception of kingdom realities, illumination, or spiritual insight. The principle here is that man does not see with the eye, the eye gives information to the mind and the mind interprets the information fed into it. The way a man sees or interprets a thing is determined by the mind, not the eye. If the

21

condition of the mind is unstable (unrenewed by God's word) the information fed into it will not be accurately interpreted. A diseased mind is a dangerous mind. The way I saw things determined whether my life was filled with light or darkness. Light signifies Godly perception, goodness, awareness of spiritual things. Darkness signifies distorted information, diseased thought patterns, an evil eye, rejection of knowledge, perception influenced by satanic interference. I needed **THE LIGHT**, illumination from the Word of God, in order to control the thoughts of my mind. God, by His Spirit, revealed to me how this was done.

II Corinthians 10:3-5

For though we walk in the flesh, we do not war after the flesh: For the weapons of our warfare are not carnal, but mighty through God to the pulling down of strongholds; Casting down imaginations, and every high thing that exalteth itself against the knowledge of God, and bringing into captivity every thought to the obedience of our Lord Jesus Christ;

Recognizing the frailty of the flesh, I began to understand that God had equipped me with superior weapons to overcome the barriers erected in my mind. These weapons were spiritual, supernatural, based on the Word of God and rooted in a strong prayer life.

Isaiah 58:6

Is not this the fast that I have chosen? to loose the bands of wickedness, to undo the heavy burdens, and to let the oppressed go free, and that ye break every yoke?

Ephesians 6:10-18

Finally, my brethren, be strong in the Lord, and in the power of his might. Put on the

*whole armour of God, that ye may be able
to stand against the wiles (strategies) of the
devil. For we wrestle not against flesh and
blood, but against principalities, against
powers, against the rulers of the darkness
of this world, against spiritual wickedness
in high places. Wherefore take unto you the
whole armour of God, that ye may be able
to withstand in the evil day, and having done
all, to stand. Stand therefore, having your
loins girt about with truth, and having on
the breastplate of righteousness; and your
feet shod with the preparation of the gospel
of peace; Above all, taking the shield of faith,
wherewith ye shall be able to quench all the
fiery darts of the wicked. And take the helmet
of salvation, and the sword of the Spirit, which
is the word of God: Praying always with all
prayer and supplication in the Spirit, and
watching thereunto with all perseverance and
supplication for all saints;*

Proverbs 4:23
*Keep (mount guard over) thy heart (soul)
with all diligence; for out of it are the issues
(forces) of life.*

God positioned and prepared me for battle and provided
the armour necessary for success. Wholeness will not
come without a battle. There were battles in my mind and
in relationships. From **Proverbs 4:23** I recognized I had to
protect my spirit by controlling who I exposed myself to, what
I saw, heard, spoke and believed and I had the responsibility
of renewing my mind. The environment I was in was critical
to my success or defeat. No longer could I associate with
people who were negative and defeated in their minds. They

could not assist me in attaining emotional healing, but they could certainly hinder my recovery.

Failure to live without any aspect of the weaponry or armour God provided would prove hazardous. God invested in me the ability to literally pull down blockades in my mind (imaginations-images of defeat, inferiority, self-pity,) that were contrary to the truth of His Word. These blockades were lies, thought patterns contrary to God's will. They were exalted against the knowledge of God (the truth). For instance, for years, I constantly worried about what people thought of me. I wanted to please everybody all the time. I wanted people to like me. Because I had no self-worth, I thought the acceptance of others was necessary and would give me self-worth. This was a stronghold in my mind. Once I realized my self-worth was in God and so valuable that God gave His Son for my deliverance, this stronghold had to crumble. How? The application is drawn from:

Proverbs 18:20-21
A man's belly shall be satisfied with the fruit of his mouth; and with the increase of his lips shall he be filled. Death and life are in the power of the tongue: and they that love it shall eat the fruit thereof.

I had been satisfied with the fruit of my mouth, the words I had been speaking. As a result I had first-hand experience with the odor of death. If I could control my life with the words of my mouth and the thoughts of my mind, no longer would I speak words conducive to death, think thoughts conducive to death and mingle with people who are consumed with destructive behavior. I truly had to abandon thoughts like, "I'll never amount to anything" or "I fail at everything." No more! I chose life, therefore, my tongue would be filled with words of life, God's life and God's Word! I had to say with my mouth, what God said about me no matter how I felt and no matter how situations appeared. This is called operating beyond emotion, which enabled me to release the power (ability) of God and bring into captivity every negative, contrary thought to the obedience of Christ. I could not allow my emotions to influence my thinking or speaking. God's ability was released through the words of my mouth, not through my emotions or reasoning faculties. Words are powerful containers of life or death. Since I was born again, I possessed the authority to speak like God in the earth. Order would be established in my life as I spoke God's Word. Speaking how I felt and what I saw had been disastrous, this was the time for me to do it God's way. As you and I live within the parameters of God's Word, operating in that pattern of behavior He has ordained for our lives we can and will overcome obstacles. We can begin to see the challenges that are normal to everyday life as character building experiences. We can change and be the glorious creatures God fashioned us to be. If we are born again, we are His ambassadors, His representatives in this earth. We are His voice to declare His will in this earth.

Isaiah 57:19
I create the fruit of the lips; Peace, peace to him that is far off, and to him that is near, saith the Lord; and I will heal him.

Psalm 103:20
Bless the Lord, ye his angels, that excel in strength, that do his commandments, hearkening unto the voice of his word.

Numbers 23:19
God is not a man, that he should lie; neither the son of man, that he should repent: hath he said, and shall he not do it? or hath he spoken, and shall he not make it good?

Romans 4:17-21
(As it is written, I have made thee a father of many nations), before him whom he believed, even God, who quickeneth the dead, and

calleth those things which be not as though they were. Who against hope believed in hope, that he might become the father of many nations, according to that which was spoken, So shall thy seed be. And being not weak in faith, he considered not his own body now dead, when he was about an hundred years old, neither yet the deadness of Sarah's womb: He staggered not at the promise of God through unbelief; but was strong in faith, giving glory to God; And being fully persuaded that, what he had promised, he was able also to perform.

The word "quicken" comes from the Greek word "zoopoieo." Translated, it means to make alive or give life to. Only the power of God could take a dead situation and make it alive and productive. Abraham believed that what God said was greater than the condition of his body and the deadness of Sarah's womb. He chose to be fully persuaded that what God vowed He would make good. Like Abraham, I chose not to consider present conditions (facts), or the effects of the past. I began to replace the negative (deadly) information with the word of God (life-giving substance--truth). What were God's thoughts concerning me?

Jeremiah 29:11-13

For I know the thoughts that I think toward you, saith the Lord, thoughts of peace, and not of evil, to give you an expected end. Then shall ye call upon me, and ye shall go and pray unto me, and I will hearken unto you. And ye shall seek me and find me, when ye shall search for me with all your heart.

Jeremiah 33:3

Call unto me, and I will answer thee, and shew thee great and mighty things, which thou knowest not.

Psalm 91:14-16

*Because he hath set his love upon me,
therefore will I deliver him: I will set him on
high, because he hath known my name. He
shall call upon me, and I will answer him: I
will be with him in trouble; I will deliver him,
and honour him. With long life will I satisfy
him, and shew him my salvation.*

Zephaniah 3:20

*At that time will I bring you again, even in the
time that I gather you: for I will make you a
name and a praise among all people of the
earth, when I turn back your captivity before
your eyes, saith the Lord.*

I was on God's mind (just as you are). He had thoughts of
peace concerning me and not evil. He had already ordained
the time and season for my deliverance. I had a promise from
Him. If I would call on Him, He would not only hear but He
would answer, deliver, and honor me as well. He had already
designated my purpose in life and as I set myself to seek His
face, he had the answer to every one of my questions. God
vowed to be with me in difficult times, to deliver me and reverse
my captive state before my eyes. My total self-worth was not
based upon the opinions of others, past failures, or mishaps as
I perceived. On the contrary, my self-worth was based upon
what He had accomplished for me through His Son. My self-
worth was based on who He fashioned me to be. I was formed
for His glory. As I rehearsed these truths by declaring them
daily I experienced the reward of:

Psalm 34:4

*I sought the Lord, and he heard me and
delivered me from all my fears.*

Job 22:27-28
Thou shalt make thy prayer unto him, and he shall hear thee, and thou shalt pay thy vows. Thou shalt also decree a thing, and it shall be established unto thee: and the light shall shine upon thy ways.

Indeed God was directing my life for a far greater purpose. He had an awesome plan for my life! If I would begin to seek Him, then I would find Him and discover that plan. I had to rid myself of anything that would hold me in bondage. There was something greater facing me, the call of God. I became focused, looking to Jesus, remembering His endurance for me and His reward of that endurance. I was experiencing something new, a time when the negatives (facts) of the past were irrelevant, and all my tomorrows with the Lord Jesus Christ were certain. My life had to be free of any form of contamination.

Hebrews 12:1-2
Wherefore seeing we also are compassed about with so great a cloud of witnesses, let us lay aside every weight, and the sin which doth so easily beset us, and let us run with patience the race that is set before us, Looking unto Jesus the author and finisher of our faith; for the joy that was set before him endured the cross, despising the shame and is set down at the right hand of the throne of God.

Colossians 1:12-14
Giving thanks unto the Father, which hath made us meet (fit) to be partakers of the inheritance of the saints in light: Who hath delivered us from the power of darkness, and hath translated us into the kingdom of his dear Son:...

28

My life was set apart for God. He gave me a new beginning and established me in His kingdom. He brought me from bondage to freedom and from darkness to light. He does this in all who put their trust in Him. We must abandon self pity. We must come to know that we grow in the hard places and none of us are immune to the challenges of life. It is not the challenge that dictates the future course of our lives but rather our view of the challenge and how we respond to the challenge.

CHAPTER THREE

THE WOMAN GOD CREATED (PERFECT REFLECTION)

The appropriate image of the woman God destined me to be had to be captured by every fiber of my being. It was not enough to believe what God said about me. I had to also see myself as God saw me. This would be accomplished as I searched the scriptures concerning who God fashioned woman to be and allow those scriptures, to paint images within of who I really was. I had to replace negative images with God-filled images. I found perfect reflection as I began to daily look into the mirror of God's Word. No longer could I believe the lies of my past. The devil invaded my life with negative thoughts and lies. He attempted to discredit my self-worth before my own eyes and before God day and night. If I would overcome, I had to be convinced of my salvation, be filled with God's Spirit and give myself over to daily study and live in God's Word.

Revelation 12:10-11

And I heard a loud voice saying in heaven, Now is come salvation, and strength, and the kingdom of our God, and the power of his Christ: for the accuser of our brethren is cast down, which accused them before our God day and night. And they (the righteous) overcame him (the devil) by the blood of the Lamb, and by the word of their testimony; and they loved not their lives unto death.

In spite of the strategy of the devil to destroy me, there was a higher authority referencing who I was. Never before had I realized the importance of looking within and examining myself. Why had I been so insecure? Why had I felt so ugly and intimidated by others? Why had I experienced feelings of inferiority when in a crowd of women? Why had I perceived in my own mind, everybody else should be looked up to and I be shunned and scorned? I found the answer when I looked into the mirror.

I had been influenced by the wrong information for years. I allowed myself to be gullible to a false image simply because of circumstances. I hated all that happened to me. I hated those who hurt me and I hated me. I blamed myself for what happened in the past. I must reiterate that I had never known self-love. Simply loving "me" because I was "me". I allowed the past to influence my self-worth and thus developed a poor image in my own eyes of who I was. Feeling good about myself was out of the question. **John 10:10** says: *"The thief cometh not but for to steal and to kill and to destroy, I (Jesus) am come that they might have life, and that they might have it more abundantly."* Jesus came to give me life, and life more abundantly. The devil came to steal, kill and destroy. **I Peter 5:8** says: *"Be sober, be vigilant; because your adversary the devil, as a roaring lion, walketh about, seeking whom he may devour."*

In these verses God reveals satan's objective is not simply to steal and to kill but ultimately to destroy. He had me on his "hit list" and made attempts to destroy me by planting thoughts of suicide in my mind. He made attempts to completely destroy my self-esteem. He desired ultimately to take my self-worth, and self-value. The principle underlying it all was if I did not believe in myself, it would be impossible to have faith in God. If the devil could get me to feel bad about who I was, every aspect of my life would be influenced in a negative manner.

The Lord further reveals how satan used this attempt on Jesus. In **Matthew 3:17**, *"And lo, a voice from heaven, saying, This is my beloved Son, in whom I am well pleased."* God reaffirms that Jesus is His Son. However, in **Matthew 4:1-3** *"Then was Jesus led up of the Spirit into the wilderness to be tempted of* *the devil. And when He had fasted forty days and forty nights, He was afterward an hungred. And when the tempter came to Him, he said, If thou be the Son of God, command that these stones be made bread.*" In essence the devil was saying, "if you are really the Son of God, prove it." The devil questioned what God had affirmed and attempted to plant doubt in the mind of Jesus about who He (Jesus) was. Needless to say, his attempts failed. He attempted to steal the self-esteem, the self-worth, and the awareness that Jesus had of who He was, and consequently stop Jesus' entire ministry. It's wonderful to know that Jesus did not have to prove Himself to satan. He knew who He was and walked in light of this truth. One day I captured this same awareness of who I was and who I represented. Today, I walk in the fullness of this light. The devil uses the same strategy today on many. It is clearly seen in **Genesis 3:1-5**.

The devil's attempts are the same today. He wants God's people to question their identity. "Am I really a child of God?" "Am I really a new creature?" "Does God really love me in spite of my past?" "Will I ever amount to anything?" "Will I ever overcome the effects of yesterday?" Satan tried to influence me to doubt who I was in Christ. As long as I failed to believe in me, I was useless to God, to myself, and to others. I could not possibly fulfill the call of God on my life and live the complete Christian life as long as I felt bad about myself. After all, I was God's representative in the earth, His ambassador and His mouthpiece. No longer did I attempt to prove my self-worth to others. God said He would prove me before all men. The only avenue God has to establish His kingdom in this earth is His body (the church). The only legal right He has to operate in this earth realm is through His body (saved or redeemed man). The Body of Christ must come to this realization if God's kingdom is to be established in this earth.

How do you combat constant battles in the mind? I had to act on **I Peter 5:9-10**, "*Whom (the devil) resist stedfast in the faith, knowing that the same afflictions are accomplished*

33

in your brethren that are in the world. But the God of all grace, who hath called us unto his eternal glory by Christ Jesus, after that ye have suffered a while, make you perfect, stablish, strengthen, settle you." I resisted the devil by making a decision not to meditate on negative thoughts. I had to understand that others, even Jesus, had been afflicted by the devil and because Jesus overcame, and others overcame, I too would overcome. This status of overcoming is verified in the following scriptures.

Hebrews 4:15
For we have not an high priest which cannot be touched with the feeling of our infirmities; but was in all points tempted like as we are, yet without sin.

John 16:33
These things I have spoken unto you, that in me ye might have peace. In the world ye shall have tribulation: but be of good cheer; I have overcome the world.

I John 4:4
Ye are of God, little children, and have overcome them: because greater is he that is in you, than he that is in the world.

Psalm 34:19
Many are the afflictions of the righteous: but the Lord delivereth him out of them all.

Revelation 3:21-22
To him that overcometh will I grant to sit with me in my throne, even as I also overcame, and am set down with my Father in his throne. He that hath an ear, let him hear what the Spirit saith unto the churches.

II Timothy 3:10-12

But thou hast fully known my doctrine, manner of life, purpose, faith, longsuffering, charity, patience, Persecutions, afflictions, which came unto me at Antioch, at Iconium, at Lystra; what persecutions I endured: but out of them all the Lord delivered me. Yea, and all that will live godly in Christ Jesus shall suffer persecution.

God's Word gave me a "champion's mentality" and a "winner's attitude." The concept of overcoming was rooted in me. No one enjoys problems, but a problem is only an opportunity for development and growth. A problem is an opportunity to see God at His best. A problem is a stepping stone to victory. If a person desires victory, he or she must take on a different concept about the challenges of life. Remember, adverse situations, (I choose to call them challenges), are subject to change and only opportunities for miracles. Challenges are invitations to arouse or stimulate those involved by presenting difficulties. Difficulties are overcome with proper attitude, mental discipline, knowledge, prayer, patience, and persistence. God revealed this and so many powerful truths to uncover the devil's lies, and I chose to believe the truth.

II Corinthians 4:18

While we look not at the things which are seen, but at the things which are not seen: for the things which are seen are temporal; but the things which are not seen are eternal.

Choosing to believe the truth was a matter of my will. My decision to believe God's Word would establish the course of future events, relationships, and my success in life. I chose to believe I was a member of the family of the Almighty God. I chose to believe I could win in life.

I John 3:1-3

Behold, what manner of love the Father hath bestowed upon us, that we should be called the sons (inclusive of daughters) of God: therefore the world knoweth us not, because it knew him not. Beloved, now are we the sons of God, and it doth not yet appear what we shall be: but we know that, when he shall appear, we shall be like him; for we shall see him as he is. And every man that hath this hope in him purifieth himself, even as he is pure.

I Corinthians 6:19-20

What? know ye not that your body is the temple of the Holy Ghost which is in you, which ye have of God, and ye are not your own? For ye are bought with a price: therefore glorify God in your body, and in your spirit, which are God's.

I John 4:16-17

*And we have known and believed the love that God hath to us. God is love; and he that dwelleth in love dwelleth in God, and God in him. Herein is our love made perfect, that we may have boldness in the day of judgment: because **AS HE IS, SO ARE WE IN THIS WORLD.***

God had chosen my body to be His dwelling place. He had to give me His perspective of who I was and who I am. He gave me self-worth. My relationship with Him gave me identity, purpose worth and significance. Being exposed to God's perspective, which revealed truth and knowledge, would do me no good unless I applied these truths by entering into agreement with God, seeing myself in light of them, meditating on them and disciplining myself to implement them by practical application (lifestyle). I had to live out the knowledge I was acquiring in order to be whole. I had to see myself included in the plan of God. Exposure to knowledge does not bring change. A decision, coupled with discipline, consistent effort and the power of God brings change. Let me reiterate "**CHANGE IS A CHOICE.**"

James 1:22-25
But be ye doers of the word, and not hearers only, deceiving your own selves. For if any be a hearer of the word, and not a doer, he is like unto a man beholding his natural face in a glass (mirror): For he beholdeth himself, and goeth his way, and straightway forgetteth what manner of man he was. But whoso looketh into the perfect law of liberty, and continueth therein, he being not a forgetful hearer, but a doer of the work, this man shall be blessed in his deed.

Psalm 50:23
Whoso offereth praise glorifieth me: and to him that ordereth his conversation (lifestyle) aright will I shew the salvation of God.

God said if I would order my lifestyle (conversation) by His Word, He would allow me to experience His delivering power. Daily looking into God's Word, the perfect law of liberty, kept me focused. Only a person who has been in bondage can understand what it means to experience true deliverance. Genuine and complete deliverance comes only by the power of God. Worst than bondage is a man having the keys to his own deliverance, yet lacking the knowledge of what he has and when knowledge comes he refuses to take advantage of the knowledge made available.

Romans 8:14-18

For as many as are led by the Spirit of God, they are the sons (inclusive of daughters) of God. For ye have not received the spirit of bondage again to fear; but ye have received the Spirit of adoption, whereby we cry, Abba, Father. The Spirit himself beareth witness with our spirit, that we are the children of God: And if children, then heirs; heirs of God, and joint-heirs with Christ; if so be that we suffer with him, that we may be also glorified together. For I reckon that the sufferings of this present time are not worthy to be compared with the glory which shall be revealed in us.

John 3:16-17

For God so loved the world, that He gave His only begotten Son, that whosoever believeth in Him should not perish, but have everlasting life. For God sent not His Son into the world to condemn the world; but that the world through Jesus, might be saved.

I was included. God's Son gave His life so that I could have life. The Greek word for "life" in **John 10:10** is "ZOE." Zoe means life in the highest form; absolute, pure, total, complete life or life as God lives; the God-kind of life. This life in the highest form was mine because I was indeed a new-creature and the greatest expression of the power of God is exemplified in redeemed man. I was special and had to build God's image within by positive affirmation of the woman He created me to be. That's who I really was and that's who I became. Self esteem would come as I built that Godly image within with the words of my mouth.

Daily I studied powerful scriptures concerning God's viewpoint towards His people. This reinforced the truth within.

These scripture references set my life on course for total and absolute internal healing, and will do the same for anyone willing to take God at His Word:

II Corinthians 3:17-18 (Amplified Bible)
Now the Lord is the Spirit, and where the Spirit of the Lord is, there is liberty--emancipation from bondage, freedom. And all of us as with unveiled face (because we) continued to behold (in the Word of God) as in a mirror the glory of the Lord, are constantly being transfigured in His very own image in ever increasing splendor and from one degree of glory to another; (for this comes) from the Lord (who is) the Spirit.

Ephesians 4:22-24
That ye put off concerning the former conversation (lifestyle) the old man, which is corrupt according to the deceitful lusts; And be renewed in the spirit of your mind; And that ye put on the new man, which after God is created in righteousness and true holiness.

II Corinthians 5:17
Therefore if any man (inclusive of woman) be in Christ, he is a new creature: old things are passed away; behold, all things are become new.

II Corinthians 5:20-21
Now then we are ambassadors for Christ, as though God did beseech you by us; we pray you in Christ's stead, be ye reconciled to God. For he hath made him to be sin for us, who knew no sin; that we might be made the righteousness of God in him.

Romans 5:17-18

For if by one man's offence death reigned by one; much more they which receive abundance of grace and of the gift of righteousness shall reign in life by one, Jesus Christ. Therefore as by the offence of one judgment came upon all men to condemnation; even so by the righteousness of one the free gift came upon all men unto justification of life.

God's Word brought emancipation from bondage. Daily I declared, "Father, In the name of Jesus, I thank You that I am clothed in the free gift of Your righteousness. I am innocent. I am blameless before You. I am forgiven. I am WHOLE!" The Spirit of God was within me to empower me. An awesome transformation was taking place as a result of consistent exposure to, understanding of, and adherence to God's Word. The only sure and permanent way of changing the image I had of myself was outlined so clearly. Effort combined with knowledge and the Spirit of God gave me my rightful image, my God ordained image in order that I might fulfill my God ordained purpose, predestined before my very conception.

My relationship with God gave me position, purpose, power, provision, protection, promotion (elevation in life), and responsibility. God predestined that I would be conformed to the image of His Son. He ordained me to be just like Jesus. I was being conformed into the image of His Son. The Greek word for confession is "homologeo" which means "to agree with or say the same thing God says about you and your circumstances." I simply agreed with God. **II Corinthians 1:20** says, *"For all the promises of God in Him are yea, and in Him Amen, unto the glory of God by us."* All of God's promises in Him are yes and all of His promises are true. There is nothing negative about what God's Word has to say about His people as they live in obedience to Him.

Romans 8:29-33

For whom he did foreknow, he also did predestinate to be conformed to the image of his Son, that he might be the firstborn among many brethren. Moreover whom he did predestinate, them he also called: and whom he called, them he also justified: and whom he justified, them he also glorified. What shall we then say to these things? If God be for us, who can be against us? He that spared not his own Son, but delivered him up for us all, how shall he not with him also freely give us all things? Who shall lay any thing to the charge of God's elect? It is God that justifieth.

The Holy Spirit was and is ever present with me, delivering me from any form of bondage. As I looked into the Word of God (I must emphasize daily and mirror) the lies were dispelled and I acquired the insight that God fashioned me by His very own hands. After reading **Genesis 1:27**, I begin to see myself more assuredly than ever before, as a woman possessing great worth. No, I would not be nominal, marginal, or mediocre. God designed me after Himself for Himself. What greater pattern is there in existence? Needless to say, "THERE IS NONE."

Genesis 1:27

So God created man (species of mankind-inclusive of woman) in His own image, in the image of God created he him; male and female created he them.

When God talks about "man", He is using the word generically and it means male and female. It refers to the species of mankind as opposed to animals. God created man and woman in His very own image after His likeness and blessed them. God has and always will desire His people to be blessed. The word "blessed" means honored, enjoying the bliss of God's favor and blessings.

In **Genesis 1:27**, *"God created the man and the woman exact duplicates of God."* God (in Himself) has both the masculine and feminine characteristics which we see in men and women. As God formed Adam in His image, after His likeness, He placed both masculine and feminine characteristics in him.

When God took from Adam a rib and from the rib created woman, He took the strengths of the feminine nature and placed them in woman. Woman comes from the Hebrew word Ish-shah. Ish-shah literally means she-man, womb-man, man with a womb or female man because woman was taken out of man. From the rib God took from the man, He skillfully built, formed and handcrafted woman. WOW!!! That was exciting. Never would life on this earth be the same. There was more to discover. The search was on. Yes, woman had been created in the image and likeness of the Almighty. This was not just in order that man might have someone suitable and adaptable to him, but God created the male-man and the female-man for His very own pleasure. Because God is Spirit, He does not make a distinction in gender as man does. He knew man and woman as spirit-beings before He ever clothed them with human flesh (My book "IN HIS PRESENCE" better explains this).

Genesis 2:21-23

And the Lord God caused a deep sleep to fall upon Adam, and he slept: and he took one of his ribs, and closed up the flesh instead thereof; And the rib, which the Lord God had taken from man, made he a woman, and brought her unto the man. And Adam said, This is now bone of my bones, and flesh of my flesh: she shall be called Woman, because she was taken out of Man.

Revelation 4:11

Thou art worthy, O Lord, to receive glory and honour and power: for thou hast created all things, and for thy pleasure they are and were created.

Galatians 3:28
There is neither Jew nor Greek, there is neither bond nor free, there is neither male nor female: for ye are all one in Christ Jesus.

I Corinthians 6:17
But he that is joined unto the Lord is one spirit.

John 4:24
God is a Spirit: and they that worship him must worship him in spirit and in truth.

With the hands of the God of this "universe", woman was skillfully handcrafted. The inferiority, the insecurity, the inadequacy had to go. Never again could this woman's image be tainted or scarred after such truth became hers to live by. For now, this woman, saw herself as the Father saw her.

Psalm 139:14
I will praise thee; for I am fearfully and wonderfully made: marvelous are thy works; and that my soul knoweth right well.

Psalm 8:3-6 (Amplified)
When I view and consider Your Heavens, the work of Your fingers, the moon and the stars which You have ordained and established; what is man (inclusive of the female-man), that You are mindful of him, and the son of earthborn man, that You care for him? Yet You have made him but a little lower than God and You have crowned him with glory and honor. You made him to have dominion over the works of Your hands; You have put all things under his feet.

If this did not elevate my self-esteem, nothing would. This very scripture gave me a degree of confidence in who I was that no psychologist, psychotherapist or psychiatrist could ever persuade me of. Complete confidence in who I was in Christ was the attribute and attitude I needed to experience success in life.

Ephesians 2:10 (Amplified)

For we are God's (own) handiwork (His workmanship), recreated in Christ Jesus, (born anew) that we may do those good works which God predestined (planned beforehand) for us, (taking paths which He prepared ahead of time) that we should walk in them living the good life which He prearranged and made ready for us to live.

Woman represents the work of God's hands. With all this information about who I really was, I came to love myself. Once again, I understood that God was not holding anything against me. He had forgiven me and sent His only Son, Jesus, to experience death for me so that I would never know the agony of eternal separation from Him--eternal damnation. The love of my biological father was not love but a sickness. Even though the devil interfered with me fully experiencing the parental love of my earthly father, I now experienced a love that superseded all love; a love far greater, the love of my Heavenly Father.

Romans 5:8

But God commendeth his love toward us, in that, while we were yet sinners, Christ died for us.

I looked into this verse and saw myself. God loved me (as He does all those who come to Him and put their trust in Him). I had to be of much value if He would not withhold the blood of His only Son for me. Indeed I was a new woman and a new creature. I had the nature of God and His greatness was revealed when even through tragedies He caused triumph to be the end result in my life. God loves you today and yes, you are of much value to Him. In spite of the tragedies you have experienced, triumph can be the end result for you.

Romans 8:35-39

Who shall separate us from the love of Christ? shall tribulation, or distress, or persecution, or famine, or nakedness, or peril, or sword? As it is written, For thy sake we are killed all the day long; we are accounted as sheep for the slaughter. Nay, in all these things we are more than conquerors through him that loved us. For I am persuaded, that neither death, nor life, nor angels, nor principalities, nor powers, nor things present, nor things to come, Nor height, nor depth, nor any other creature, shall be able to separate us from the love of God, which is in Christ Jesus our Lord.

My position in Him was secure and His love unending. My sins and iniquities He remembered no more. (**Hebrews 10:17**) Life for me had meaning and life had purpose. God mapped out His perfect direction, His perfect plan for my life through His Word. He gave me identity. Decayed dreams, and shattered emotions were dispelled. God's Word brought illumination. His Word brought light and light totally eradicated darkness.

I Peter 2:9-10

But ye are a chosen generation, a royal priesthood, an holy nation, a peculiar people; that ye should shew forth the praises of him who hath called you out of darkness into his marvelous light: Which in time past were not a people, but are now the people of God: which had not obtained mercy, but now have obtained mercy.

45

The choice was mine. I decided that God's call on my life would not be unfulfilled. My life would be a living testimony of the most magnificent display of the power of God to heal the emotionally shattered, spiritually wounded, and the broken and battered. My life would exemplify the exhibition of His power that is great and intense. All I have exposed in this book opens me up for criticism, but the criticism can be endured, in order that women by the countless thousands will come to see themselves as God sees them. Women can rise above the despair, guilt, shame and hopelessness that the adverse experiences of life can leave them in.

With the unveiling of my life, other women will walk from bondage to freedom. For too long the haunting effects of rape, pregnancy before marriage, molestation, divorce, incest, verbal, mental and physical abuse, racial pressures and so much more have been shoved under the carpet. Now is the time for freedom. Today is the day to discover how to be a whole person, a complete woman, permanently, with no fear, no shame concerning the hideous attempts of the devil to haunt women with the mishaps of yesterday.

Yes, I have shared what once was painful and shameful information. Since I am free, how can I not share with others in order that they might come to know freedom and wholeness just because of what the critics will say? The critics would have something to say even if I did not reveal the contents in this book. To put it frankly, even they need to experience wholeness. People who constantly criticize and find fault with others have not experienced complete wholeness and are seeking to fill a void in their own lives. I have their answer. "Woman Be Whole" will not destroy my reputation. Remember, I have identity in God that not even the most brilliant of critics can destroy. The following promise from God will always prevail in my life.

Isaiah 54:14-17
In righteousness shalt thou be established:
thou shalt be far from oppression; for thou

*shalt not fear: and from terror; for it shall
not come near thee. Behold, they shall surely
gather together, but not by ME: whosoever
shall gather together against thee shall fall for
thy sake. Behold, I have created the smith that
bloweth the coals in the fire, and that bringeth
forth an instrument for his work; and I have
created the waster to destroy. No weapon
that is formed against thee shall prosper;
and every tongue that shall rise against thee
in judgment thou shalt condemn. This is the
heritage of the servants of the Lord, and their
righteousness is of me,* **SAITH THE LORD.**

I have not written this book for popularity, but by the inspiration of the Holy Spirit for the internal healing of every emotionally scarred individual. The principles outlined in this book will not only work for women, but men as well.

II Timothy 3:16-17
*All scripture is given by inspiration of God,
and is profitable for doctrine, for reproof, for
correction, for instruction in righteousness:
That the man of God (inclusive of woman)
may be perfect, thoroughly furnished unto all
good works.*

The word "inspiration" comes from a Greek word "theopneustos," which means God-breathed. The contents in this book have been divinely influenced by the Spirit of God to bring deliverance and wholeness to women all over the world. I am sure many of you reading this book have a story that is shameful, horrid, perhaps frightening to say the least. God is concerned about you and I have prayed for you. Those of you reading this book are in God's heart; you are on His mind. It is not by accident that you are reading this material. God has ordained this book a tool of ministry for you. You are not a mistake. Your life has purpose.

You have purpose and this is your opportunity for change. I would like to challenge you at this very moment. You have nothing to lose and everything to gain. Why not receive Jesus as Savior (if you have not) and allow Him to transform your very life?

You can not change yesterday but you can set the course of your tomorrows with Him. Why not start afresh? He is the only one I know who gives you a fresh beginning and totally discards your past. It's really as though the failures, the mistakes, and the nightmares never occurred. He loves you particularly and yes **"YOU CAN EXPERIENCE HIS BEST TODAY."** Remember, the first step begins with a decision. Change is a choice and the choice is yours. You can choose to overcome or you can choose to fail. Failure is not automatic, and can only be evident in your life if you choose not to succeed. Change is a decision you must make which leads you to the path of success. You can choose to excel or accept defeat. You can choose to be made whole or you can choose ultimately to experience eternal torment. Whatever you choose, the choice is yours alone. It does not matter what has happened yesterday or even what others think. What matters now is what you will do with the knowledge you have received TODAY!

Psalm 139:1-5

O Lord, thou hast searched me, and known me. Thou knowest my downsitting and mine uprising, thou understandest my thought afar off. Thou compassest my path and my lying down, and art acquainted with all my ways. For there is not a word in my tongue, but, lo, O Lord, thou knowest it altogether. Thou has beset me behind and before, and laid thine hand upon me.

II Corinthians 3:2

Ye are our epistle (letter) written in our hearts, known and read of all men.

II Corinthians 3:5

*Not that we are sufficient of our selves to think
any thing as of ourselves; but our sufficiency
is of God;...*

No longer did I feel nasty, dirty, ugly, or unclean after
receiving God's viewpoint of me. My sufficiency, confidence
and adequacy were of God. He had set me apart for His very
own use and I had been cleansed by the washing of the water by
the Word. I represented the "untainted" Bride of Christ.

Ephesians 5:26-27

*That He might sanctify (set apart) and cleanse
it (the church--body of believers) with the
washing of water by the word, That he might
present it to himself a glorious church, not
having spot, or wrinkle, or any such thing;
but that it should be holy and without blemish.*

The words I read in **Jeremiah 1:4-5** became alive within me.
I took every verse literally as my very own. You must do the
same.

Jeremiah 1:4-5

*Then the word of the Lord came unto me,
saying, Before I formed thee in the belly I
knew thee; and before thou camest forth out
of the womb I sanctified thee, and I ordained
thee a prophet unto the nations.*

God had not been the cause of the mishaps in my life, but
He was great enough to heal me internally and accomplish an
even greater purpose for my life. Satan's assault on my life was
intended to destroy. God's delivering power came to heal me
and restore wholeness. This made better sense to me when I
understood it was not God's perfect will for His Son, the Lord
Jesus Christ, to experience the brutality, mockery, and death that

He did. God's perfect will was that Adam and Eve obey Him to the fullest and live on earth eternally in the original state He created them subduing and having dominion on planet earth.

However, since they sinned and caused all men to experience separation from the Father, God had a plan. A plan by which His eternal purpose would still be fulfilled in spite of Adam and Eve's willful disobedience and the strategy of the enemy (satan) to rule the earth and its inhabitants.

Hebrews 2:9-11

But we see Jesus, who was made a little lower than the angels for the suffering of death, crowned with glory and honour; that he by the grace of God should taste death for every man. For it became him, for whom are all things, and by whom are all things, in bringing many sons unto glory, to make the captain of their salvation perfect through sufferings. For both he that sanctifieth (Jesus) and they who are sanctified (those who receive Jesus) are all of one: for which cause he is not ashamed to call them brethren.

Philippians 2:5-11

Let this mind be in you, which was also in Christ Jesus: Who, being in the form of God, thought it not robbery to be equal with God: But made himself of no reputation, and took upon him the form of a servant, and was made in the likeness of men: And being found in fashion as a man, he humbled himself, and became obedient unto death, even the death of the cross. Wherefore God also hath highly exalted him, and given him a name which is above every name: That at the name of Jesus every knee should bow, of things in heaven,

*and things in earth, and things under the
earth; And that every tongue should confess
that Jesus Christ is Lord, to the glory of God
the Father.*

The devil thought he had won when he influenced evil men to murder Jesus. On the contrary, he lost. Not only did Jesus get up from the grave, but also many lives have been established with Him in the kingdom of God. Many have come to receive Him as Lord and Savior. Spiritual death (separation from God) entered the earth because of sin. Jesus had to experience separation from His Father because there is only one place for sin and that place is the "grave". We have redemption through His blood and forgiveness of every sin past, present and future.

Colossians 1:14
*In whom we have redemption through his
blood, even the forgiveness of sins.*

Galatians 2:20
*I am crucified with Christ: nevertheless I
live; yet not I, but Christ liveth in me: and
the life which I now live in the flesh I live by
the faith of the Son of God, who loved me, and
gave himself for me.*

Colossians 2:15
*And having spoiled principalities and powers,
he made a shew of them openly, triumphing
over them in it.*

Romans 8:10-16
*And if Christ be in you, the body is dead
because of sin; but the Spirit is life because
of righteousness. But if the Spirit of him that
raised up Jesus from the dead dwell in you, he
that raised up Christ from the dead shall also*

*quicken your mortal bodies by his Spirit that
dwelleth in you. Therefore, brethren, we are
debtors, not to the flesh, to live after the flesh.
For if ye live after the flesh, ye shall die: but
if ye through the Spirit do mortify the deeds of
the body, ye shall live. For as many as are led
by the Spirit of God, they are the sons of God.
For ye have not received the spirit of bondage
again to fear; but ye have received the Spirit
of adoption, whereby we cry Abba, Father.
The Spirit himself beareth witness with our
spirit, that we are the children of God:....*

GOD WAS, IS AND ALWAYS will be great enough to allow
evil to exist for a season and still not be hindered in accomplishing
His eternal purpose in the lives of His people. It is the thief (the
devil) who comes to steal, kill and ultimately to destroy. Jesus
came that we might have life and have it more abundantly (**John
10:10**). It was not enough for Jesus to purchase life eternally for
us with His blood, but His blood also purchased a life filled with
the blessings of God to be enjoyed today--**NOW**.

Isaiah 46:9-10
*Remember the former things of old: for I
am God, and there is none else; I am God,
and there is none like me, Declaring the end
from the beginning, and from ancient times
the things that are not yet done, saying, My
counsel shall stand, and I will do all my
pleasure.*

God declared the end result for my life from the beginning.
His counsel (His Pre-determined Will) would prevail no matter
what challenges I encountered. My healing came progressively.
It began after I received Jesus Christ as my Savior and Lord.
Even though I did not have all the knowledge for this healing
to be completed in me, it still began. As knowledge became

available my healing progressed. I could only walk in light of the knowledge that I had. That knowledge was shallow and limited. Where there is no knowledge, destruction is inevitable. God says even when knowledge is made available it will do an individual no good unless it is applied appropriately. The Word of God reveals truth (complete knowledge). Rejection of God's Word is rejection of God.

Hosea 4:6
My people are destroyed for lack of knowledge: because thou hast rejected knowledge, I will also reject thee, that thou shalt be no priest to me: seeing thou hast forgotten the law of thy God, I will also forget thy children.

My healing was not physical, as with many of you, but it required just as much attention as a terminal ailment. My condition, as with many who will read this book, was acute; it was paralyzing. If not dealt with properly and promptly the results would be fatal. What prescription can be recommended for scars and wounds that run so emotionally deep that an individual can be carried to the grave with no sign of a physical ailment? The only successful prescription I can recommend is the one I know truly heals. The Bible says, "God's Word is Medicine."

Proverbs 4:22
For they (God's words) are life unto those that find them, and health to all their flesh.

Proverbs 17:22
A merry heart doeth good like a medicine: but a broken spirit drieth the bones.

I recommend the Word of God. It took more than natural human strength, reasoning, or determination of will to totally effect a healing in me. I had been enslaved and tormented within for years. No "power of positive thinking" techniques

THE WOMAN GOD CREATED
THE WOMAN GOD CREATED
THE WOMAN GOD CREATED

or secular solutions were adequate enough to bring about the cure needed. Someone greater, **"THE MASTER PHYSICIAN, THE MASTER PSYCHIATRIST, THE MASTER HEALER AND CREATOR,"** completed the process. You can become acquainted with Him as I did and receive your healing today.

CHAPTER FOUR

JOURNEY TO WHOLENESS

M any of you reading this book desire to experience wholeness or know someone who needs to be a whole or complete person. Again I say, "This is the time of decision." You can begin your journey to wholeness by capturing the principles shared throughout these pages or elect to acquire wholeness by some other means, which may prove void of the results you so desperately need. Allow me to emphasize, "I am not against physicians." However, even they admit encountering illnesses (physical and mental) for which they have no cure or answer. You have been looking for the catalyst for internal change. This book presents that catalyst straight from the "MASTER PHYSICIAN" (He who gave the Spirit--Life Force, fashioned the Human Body and provided for the Soul). Surely "HE" would know more about "HIS CREATION" than any one else.

Genesis 2:7
And the Lord God formed man of the dust of the ground, and breathed into his nostrils the breath of life; and man became a living soul.

God formed man from the dust of the ground and blew "HIS" breath into man. The breath represented the life of God entering into the man HE created. It was after God blew His breath into man that he (created man) became a living soul. Only God can take nothing and perform a miracle. Only God can take brokenness and worthlessness and create something or someone of priceless value. That word create is so powerful because it comes from the Hebrew word "bara" which means to bring into being or cause to exist.

The contents I have shared up to this point are not fictitious, but real life situations. I have not shared fantasy but fact. This chapter exposes the criteria by which I became whole, step by step.

There are people from all walks of life who have already concluded that it is not marriage, children, social status, academic or political achievements, or the lack of, that can bring a sense of wholeness. Many with all of the above and more have chosen to exit this life by suicide. There must be more to wholeness and the enjoyment of life than materialistic wealth and social standing.

What is wholeness? Wholeness is the state of being physically sound and healthy, emotionally sound and spiritually sound in order to enjoy life to the maximum (life in the highest form) regardless of circumstances; the acquisition of things or achievements.

Homo Sapiens (mankind, male/female) are Spirit Beings, who live in physical bodies, and possess souls. The Soul represents the seat of the mind, will, imagination, desires, and emotions. The Spirit of man is the real person. This Spirit and Soul will live on after physical death, either eternally in heaven or eternally in hell (based upon acceptance or rejection of the Lord Jesus Christ).

The spirit relates to spiritual things (for example, God, angels, etc.); those things, which cannot be verified by the senses, the flesh, or the mind. The Physical Body enables mankind to function on planet earth and relates to natural or physical things. The soul allows man to reason things out, to imagine, to think, exercise the power of the will to choose and to express emotion and feeling.

Wholeness can be lacking in all of these areas, or one of these areas. To be whole physically, simply means you are healthy and unrestricted by physical ailments or handicaps. If a person has never accepted Jesus Christ as Savior, he or she lacks spiritual wholeness. No individual can be spiritually whole as long as spiritual death is evident. I cannot take for granted that spiritual death is understood by all readers, therefore, let me define this condition.

To be spiritually dead means to be separated from God, void of a relationship with God due to a sin-nature, and subject to eternal torment (eternal damnation). A person can be physically alive and yet dead spiritually, because where the sin nature prevails, the nature or life of God can not co-exist.

The process by which a person can be delivered from this condition is called salvation or being born again (the new birth). The word "salvation" means deliverance; deliverance from a sin nature (the nature of the devil) to the nature of God. A person who experiences salvation may be referred to as a Christian, a believer, a child of God, a redeemed man or woman.

Romans 10:9-13

That if thou shalt confess with thy mouth the Lord Jesus, and shalt believe in thine heart that God hath raised him from the dead thou shalt be saved. For with the heart man believeth unto righteousness; and with the mouth confession is made unto salvation. For the scripture saith, Whosoever believeth on him shall not be ashamed. For there is no difference between the Jew and the Greek: for the same Lord over all is rich unto all that call upon him. For whosoever shall call upon the name of the Lord shall be saved.

God is no respecter of persons and though many find it hard to believe, He has no favorites. He is not partial. Regardless of what has taken place in life, you can be made spiritually sound and spiritually whole. Are you willing to believe in your heart that Jesus died particularly for you? Are you willing to confess with your mouth that you desire Him to govern your life from this moment on? If you are, God is willing to establish the course of your life from this moment on with a new beginning (a fresh start).

Praying this simple prayer starts your relationship with Him.

Dear God, in the name of Jesus, I believe Jesus was born of the virgin Mary and that

He hung, bled and died on Calvary, especially for me. I further believe that He arose from the dead and is alive today, seated on your right hand. Dear God, I desire wholeness in my spirit, my soul and my body. Forgive me for all my past mistakes, even as I forgive those who have offended, wounded or hurt me in any fashion. I invite You to come into my heart and make me a new creature, one possessing your nature. You said if I confess with my mouth the Lord Jesus, and believe in my heart that you raised Him from the dead, I would be saved. I believe your word and receive Jesus as Lord and Savior of my life. I turn my back on my old way of living, my old way of thinking and old way of speaking. I renouce any and every way by which satan has claimed ownership of me. From this very moment I am a new person, a whole person, a child of God, with the life of God. I am no longer spiritually dead. Thank you Father, I am saved; I am delivered. Now fill me with your Spirit and teach me how to live a life pleasing to You. I ask you to direct me to a Bible believing, Bible teaching church in order that I may learn of You more perfectly. In Jesus name, I receive by faith, Amen!

Now that you have prayed this prayer, you are a member of God's family. You are born again and entitled to all the benefits God has promised His children, as revealed in His Word. You may not feel saved. You may not feel like a child of God, even as I didn't, but you received Jesus not by emotions, feelings or reasoning. You received Jesus into your heart based upon truth, God's Word. Even though now you are spiritually whole, which is instant, your soul and body must be dealt with. Becoming

58

spiritually whole does not transform your soul or body. Now the work begins.

Remember, it is possible to be spiritually whole, sound and complete, and yet be in bondage in the soul (seat of the mind, will and emotions) and even in the body. Man is Spirit. He lives in a Physical Body. He has a Soul.

As I stated earlier, before being born into the family of God, every person has a sin nature which separates him or her from God. The Bible clearly reveals that man is born in sin and shaped in iniquity. This is so because the sin nature was passed on to man after Adam and Eve sinned or disobeyed God. Therefore, there is a need for every individual to experience spiritual wholeness, salvation or deliverance. Each person walking on planet earth is a sinner until Jesus is made Lord of his or her life. Jesus being "LORD" simply means that a person allows the Word of God to be the governing factor in every area of life without compromise or deviation.

Romans 5:12
Wherefore, as by one man sin entered into the world, and death by sin; and so death (spiritual death--separation from God) passed upon all men, for that all have sinned:....

As long as a person has this sin nature (void of the life of God), he or she is programmed by what is known as satanic or demonic influence. God's life within gives man a restraining force, the Holy Spirit. A person who is spiritually dead has the nature of the devil. The soul is under the influence of that nature. After being born again (spiritually whole), the recipient of this new experience cannot attempt to judge himself or herself by this soul which had been governed for years by a sin nature that was under the influence of satan.

When you are born again you have the nature of God. However, you must nourish yourself with new information. This new information is God's Word and is the essential element by which the soul must be renewed. In order to transform this soul that has been under satanic rule, the old data stored there must be driven out by the new. Why is this process so vital? Again, we recall the following scripture:

Proverbs 23:7
For as he thinketh in his heart, so is he.

What you believe about yourself and say about yourself will affect your attitude towards God, toward others, yourself, and life in general. Remember in the earlier chapters how, even though I was saved, I still had a poor image of who I was. Not only was my image of who I was distorted, but it affected my relationship with others who knew nothing of what I had experienced in life.

Matthew 16:16-18
And Simon Peter answered and said, Thou art the Christ, the Son of the living God. And Jesus answered and said unto him, Blessed art thou, Simon Barjona: for flesh and blood hath not revealed it unto thee, but my Father, which is in heaven. And I say also unto thee, That thou art Peter, and upon this rock I will build my church; and the gates of hell shall not prevail against it.

Man can only know the truth about himself, God, life, others, and so much more as he reads the Word of God, studies the Word of God, believes the Word of God, and lives the Word of God. God gives the revelation (insight) and establishes our lives by it. The very counsels of darkness (satanic interference) cannot stand against the truth of God. It is the truth that makes men free. To "make" is a gradual process. To become whole in the soul is progressive. A little at a time, we shed the thoughts of the past and the emotions tied to those thoughts. Gradually, we take on the thinking of "One" who is greater. Remember the metamorphosis we discussed.

Luke 21:19
In your patience possess ye your souls.

Matthew 11:28-30
Come unto me, all ye that labour and are heavy laden, and I will give you rest. Take my yoke upon you, and learn of me; for I am meek and lowly in heart: and ye shall find rest unto your souls. For my yoke is easy and my burden is light.

Psalm 23:3
He restores my soul...

Hebrews 10:35-36 (Amplified)
Do not, therefore, fling away your fearless confidence, for it carries a great and glorious compensation or reward. For you have need of stedfast patience and endurance, so that you may perform and fully accomplish the will of God, and thus receive and carry away (and enjoy to the full) what is promised.

By patient endurance, you will mount guard over your soul (mind, will and emotions) and establish complete oneness with God. Have you ever wondered why patience and endurance are necessary for a runner? Endurance is essential to mental toughness because the competition is tremendous. It keeps the runner from quitting prematurely. Patience is essential because it undergirds endurance. The runner understands it is only a matter of time before reaching the finish line. He has already paced himself and understands that he will not finish the race all at once, but he will finish. It will take a stride at a time. Each stride brings him closer to winning, closer to victory, closer to the finish line. He is focused and will not be detoured by side-line distractions. The reward at the end is sure if he can endure. Patience anchors him while endurance keeps him moving toward victory.

Joshua 1:7

Only be thou strong and very courageous, that thou mayest observe to do according to all the law, which Moses my servant commanded thee: turn not from it to the right hand or to the left, that thou mayest prosper whithersoever thou goest.

I Corinthians 2:16

For who hath known the mind of the Lord, that he may instruct him? But we have the mind of Christ.

God's Word reveals the end result. The truth about who you are becomes a reality as you rehearse who you are from the Word of God. Every person must allow the mind of Christ to rule. The Bible reveals the mind of God. This is "THE MIND" man's mind must be renewed by. You can change any thought anytime you want. If you dwell on negative thoughts from your past, they will keep you from developing confidence in yourself and limit you throughout your life. You can change them in a split second and begin to believe in yourself and live the life God has planned for you. For instance, if a thought comes such as this: "you'll never be able to accomplish anything of worth in life." Do not meditate on that negative thought. Do not speak it. That thought will die prematurely if you resist giving birth to it with your mouth. Immediately speak out of your mouth what is in the "MIND OF GOD--THE BIBLE". We do not have to allow negative words, critical talk or corrupt communication to fall from our lips.

Phillipians 4:13

I can do all things through Christ who strengtheneth me.

In essence, you just practiced the renewal of the mind process. In a split second you made the decision to allow God's Word to override that negative data that has dictated the course of your life in times past. Another example, perhaps you had an abortion at an early age in life and the devil brings this old information up to torment you and rob you of the peace of God. Remember that old person is dead, you are a new creature with a new beginning. Meditate on the truth and speak the truth from God's perspective. You are innocent. Begin to say, "Father I thank You that my sins and iniquities you remember no more." You don't have to meditate on the negatives of the past. The following scriptures are greater than any mistake of the past.

Romans 8:1-2
There is therefore now no condemnation to them which are in Christ Jesus, who walk not after the flesh, but after the Spirit. For the law of the Spirit of life in Christ Jesus hath made me free from the law of sin and death.

John 5:24
Verily, verily, I say unto you, He that heareth my word, and believeth on him that sent me, hath everlasting life, and shall not come into condemnation; but is passed from death (spiritual death) unto life.

III John 1:2
Beloved, I wish above all things that thou mayest prosper and be in health, even as thy soul prospereth.

In these verses we see God's perspective concerning His people. In **III John 1:2**, John says his prayer for every believer is that they experience wholeness in the trinity of their person.

God dismissed all charges against those who have received Jesus as Lord and Savior. Jesus Christ brought life (Spirit of life). All those who live not after the dictates of the flesh but after the dictates of the Holy Spirit enjoy this life. Those who reject

Jesus Christ experience the penalty of sin which is death (eternal separation from God--the law of sin and death).

It is in the arena of the mind that we experience battle after battle. The devil's only avenue into our lives always originates in the mind. His aim is to persuade us to speak how we feel, what it looks like and the negative thoughts he subtly plants in the mind. He understands death and life are in the power of the tongue. He knows we'll experience just what we say. This is why I believe Jesus gave one of the most powerful revelations concerning our thoughts.

Matthew 6:31
Therefore take no thought, saying,....

Jesus emphasized the importance of trusting in God and not worrying about how we would survive from one day to another. He was not telling us to refrain from wise planning; however, He was emphasizing the importance of our establishing priorities. Seeking the kingdom must be paramount. This simply means God wants man to establish a relationship with Him first and live daily by the principles He has outlined in His Word.

When Jesus told His disciples to "take no thought, saying...," He was talking about speaking out of anxious concern. A negative thought, or a thought initiated by worry or lack of trust in God will die unborn if never given life or a legal right to live by speaking it. If we refrain from speaking the foolishness that comes to mind, it will die without producing in our lives. Jesus said, "take no thought saying." Don't embrace a thought and speak it just because it enters your mind. I don't have to remind you that much of what we think, we don't speak. On the other hand, much of what we think, we do speak. Let's decide today that those thoughts we don't want to yield a return in our lives, we will not speak. We will follow the example Jesus taught His disciples, realizing this it was not just for them only, but for us as well.

We have examined how to be made spiritually whole. We have examined how the soul becomes whole (renewed). Now the physical body (flesh man) must be controlled. God gives specific instructions concerning the body.

Romans 12:1-3
I beseech you therefore, brethren, by the mercies of God, that ye present your bodies a living sacrifice, holy, acceptable unto God, which is your reasonable service. And be not conformed to this world: but be ye transformed by the renewing of your mind, that ye may prove what is that good, and acceptable, and perfect will of God. For I say, through the grace given unto me, to every man that is among you, not to think of himself more highly than he ought to think; but to think soberly, according as God hath dealt to every man the measure of faith.

I Corinthians 9:27 (Amplified)
But (like a boxer) I buffet my body--handle it roughly, discipline it by hardships and subdue it, for fear that after proclaiming to others the gospel and things pertaining to it, I myself should become unfit, not stand the test, and be unapproved and rejected (as a counterfeit).

Ephesians 4:22-24
That ye put off concerning the former conversation the old man, which is corrupt according to the deceitful lusts; And be renewed in the spirit of your mind; And that ye put on the new man, which after God is created in righteousness and true holiness.

Acts 24:16 (Amplified)
Therefore, I always exercise and discipline myself--mortifying my body (deadening my

carnal affections, bodily appetites and worldly desires), endeavoring in all respects--to have a clear (unshaken, blameless) conscience, void of offense toward God and toward men.

I Thessalonians 4:1-5 (Amplified)
Furthermore, brethren, we beg and admonish you in (virtue of our union with) the Lord Jesus, that (you follow the instructions which) you learned from us about how you ought to walk so as to please and gratify God, as indeed you are doing; that you do so even more and more abundantly--attaining yet greater perfection in living this life. For you know what charges and precepts we gave you on the authority and by the inspiration of the Lord Jesus. For this is the will of God, that you should be consecrated--separated and set apart for pure and holy living: that you should abstain and shrink from all sexual vice; that each one of you should know how to possess (control, manage) his own body (in purity, separated from things profane and) in consecration and honor, not (to be used) in the passion of lust, like the heathen who are ignorant of the true God and have no knowledge of His will...

It is amazing that after salvation the body will attempt to do everything it did before salvation. This is why we must put restraints on the flesh. By this, I mean we must literally exercise control in every situation. If an individual was a "smoker" before salvation of the spirit and renewal of the mind, the flesh will desire to continue this act. The individual must first makes a decision to change. The next step is to use discipline and control to overcome this behavior. By all means the Holy Spirit is present to assist in overcoming all challenges with the desires of the flesh. Will there be a battle? What does the Bible say?

Galatians 5:16-17

This I say then, Walk in the Spirit, and ye shall not fulfil the lust of the flesh. For the flesh lusteth against the Spirit, and the Spirit against the flesh: and these are contrary the one to the other: so that ye cannot do the things that ye would.

The flesh will war against the recreated spirit's desire to live holy, but if we will yield to the Word of God and not the flesh we will overcome. (My teaching series, "Whose Winning This War", will greatly benefit all those who struggle with gaining the mastery over this flesh).

James 4:7

Submit yourselves therefore to God. Resist the devil, and he will flee from you.

Romans 6:11-14

Likewise reckon ye also yourselves to be dead indeed unto sin, but alive unto God through Jesus Christ our Lord. Let not sin therefore reign in your mortal body, that ye should obey it in the lusts thereof. Neither yield ye your members as instruments of unrighteousness unto sin: but yield yourselves unto God, as those that are alive from the dead, and your members as instruments of righteousness unto God. For sin shall not have dominion over you: for ye are not under the law, but under grace.

"**Renewal of the soul, development of the spirit** and **control of the flesh**", cultivates man's relationship with God.

67

This process of change may present some discomfort, but the end result will cause a distinct difference and rewarding future. Man's obedience to God, consistent endurance coupled with discipline, will bring him to full development and complete wholeness.

Satan is determined to stop any positive moves we attempt to make. Determination, discipline, self motivation, spiritual tenacity, and mental toughness with knowledge of real purpose and real desire will cause us to be victorious. Knowledge can affect our will, and influence our will but information cannot make us do anything. In order for change to occur, you and I must become so dissatisfied with where we are in life and what we are until we open ourselves up to God for change. Surely, if anyone could make a notable difference in our lives God not only is able, but willing as well. The discomfort that accompanies change is minimal when you consider the long-term results. I had been hurting for a long time but the discomfort changing presented was not nearly as traumatic as the bondage I had been in for years.

Perhaps many think, "I have been tormented in my mind and emotions for so long, it's too late. I'll never be able to think as God thinks." It is not too late. You may feel "I have been drinking for years. I am hooked." I must encourage you by saying, "**NO CONDITION IS BEYOND THE POWER OF GOD TO TRANSFORM.**" This renewal of the mind and control of the flesh will not be accomplished by you alone. Yes, your consent and determination to change is necessary, but you will be assisted by the **HOLY SPIRIT**. He is the "HELPER, REVEALER OF TRUTH, TEACHER, GUIDE, STRENGTHENER AND SO MUCH MORE!!!" He comes to teach you and supply the power you need in every area of life. Allow the following truths to be your motivation for change.

Jeremiah 32:27
Behold, I am the Lord, the God of all flesh: is there any thing too hard for Me?

John 14:16-17

*And I will pray the Father, and he shall give
you another Comforter, that he may abide with
you for ever; Even the Spirit of truth; whom
the world cannot receive, because it seeth him
not, neither knoweth him: but ye know him;
for he dwelleth with you, and shall be in you.*

You have become personally acquainted with the God who
not only heals the body, but the soul as well. He has elevated
you to a new level of living. He has promised to give you ONE
who will be with you forever. That person is the Holy Spirit and
He is the power of God. He comes to bring order and structure
into your life if you are willing to invite Him in and follow His
leading. He will be your best friend as you "JOURNEY TO
WHOLENESS." Allow me to further introduce Him to you
as the Comforter. The word Comforter comes from the Greek
word Parakletos which means "called to one's side." He is not
only called to one's side, He has chosen to make your body His
home.

Your first experience with Him came when you received
Jesus as Savior of your life.

I Corinthians 12:13

*For by one Spirit are we all baptized into
one body, whether we be Jews or Gentiles,
whether we be bond or free; and have been
made to drink into one Spirit.*

I Corinthians 6:17

But he that is joined unto the Lord is one spirit.

The moment you received Jesus into your heart the Holy
Spirit baptized you into the family of God. Immediately your
human spirit was recreated as the Holy Spirit imparted the nature
of God to you. You became a new creature with the life and
nature of Almighty God. He made you alive to spiritual things.

69

He made you spiritually whole and confirmed this new ownership
by setting His seal upon your spirit.

Ephesians 1:13
*In whom ye also trusted, after that ye heard
the word of truth, the gospel of your salvation:
in whom also after that ye believed, ye were
sealed with that Holy Spirit of promise.*

Now that you are saved and sealed by the Holy Spirit,
God wants you to be filled with the Holy Spirit. This is an
experience that takes place after salvation. Let me emphasize
that the moment you received Jesus as Savior the Holy Spirit
did come to live within you. Now He wants to empower you so
that you experience God's power in a dimension you have never
experienced before.

Acts 1:8
*But ye shall receive power, after that the
Holy Ghost is come upon you: and ye shall
be witnesses unto me both in Jerusalem, and
in all Judaea, and in Samaria, and unto the
uttermost part of the earth.*

Acts 2:4
*And they were all filled with the Holy
Ghost,and began to speak with other tongues,
as the Spirit gave them utterance.*

Praying this simple prayer and receiving the Holy Spirit in
His fullness by faith is all that is required after salvation:

**Heavenly Father, I have received Jesus as
Lord of my life. I am sealed by the power of
your Spirit and desire all that you have for
me. I ask you Father, in the name of Jesus,
to fill me with the Holy Spirit, empower me
to be a credible witness and give me the same**

evidence of this experience that I have seen in your word. I desire to communicate with you more perfectly and receive the fullness of the Holy Spirit by faith and all that accompanies Him, in the name of Jesus, Amen.

Now you are fully equipped. You don't have to succumb to the misfortunes of the past. You are a new creature, with a new beginning, a new lifestyle and the power of God to live for Him as a credible witness.

Ephesians 2:1-10

And you hath he quickened (made alive) who were dead in trespasses and sins; wherein in time past ye walked according to the course of this world, according to the prince of the power of the air, the spirit that now worketh in the children of disobedience: Among whom also we all had our conversation in times past in the lusts of our flesh, fulfilling the desires of the flesh and of the mind; and were by nature the children of wrath, even as others. But God, who is rich in mercy, for his great love wherewith he loved us, even when we were dead in sins, hath quickened us together with Christ, (by grace ye are saved;) and hath raised us up together, and made us sit together in heavenly places in Christ Jesus: that in the ages to come he might shew the exceeding riches of his grace in his kindness toward us through Christ Jesus. For by grace are ye saved through faith; and that not of yourselves: it is the gift of God: not of works, lest any man should boast. For we are his workmanship, created in Christ Jesus unto good works, which God hath before ordained that we should walk in them.

God has quickened you. He has made you alive spiritually by imparting to you His nature and His life. Not only has He given you spiritual wholeness, but the preceding verses say, He has raised you up together, and made you sit together in heavenly places in Christ Jesus. This refers to position. God has promoted you and elevated you with Christ Jesus. He does not hold your past against you. He sees you as righteous, covered by the blood of His Son. He has given you authority to take your rightful place and enjoy the benefits of being in the family of God.

John 1:12

But as many as received Him, to them gave he power to become the sons of God, even to them that believe on His name:

Now let's explore this ministry of wholeness by considering some incidents in the Bible.

Matthew 15:21-28

Then Jesus went thence, and departed into the coasts of Tyre and Sidon. And, behold, a woman of Canaan came out of the same coasts, and cried unto him, saying, Have mercy on me, O Lord, thou son of David; my daughter is grievously vexed with a devil. But he answered her not a word. And his disciples came and besought him, saying, Send her away; for she crieth after us. But he answered and said, I am not sent but unto the lost sheep of the house of Israel. Then came she and worshipped him, saying, Lord, help me. But he answered and said, It is not meet to take the children's bread, and to cast it to dogs. And she said, Truth, Lord: yet the dogs eat of the crumbs which fall from their masters' table. Then Jesus answered and said unto her, O woman, great is thy faith: be it unto thee even

as thou wilt. And her daughter was made
whole from that very hour.

There was an occasion in the Bible when a Syrophenician woman's daughter needed spiritual and emotional healing. Her condition was not of a physical nature because there's no reference of a handicap or physical disease. She was tormented by the devil indicating a spiritual and emotional problem. The mother cried out to Jesus one day for help. It appeared that Jesus just ignored her. His disciples encouraged Him to send the woman away for she was a nuisance. Somehow this woman of Canaan possessed the tenacity and determination to continue in her efforts despite the disciples' ploy to get rid of her. You, too, must persevere in spite of obstacles. God is no respecter of persons. He already knows what you need and what He will do even as He knew what He would do for the Syrophenician woman and her daughter.

Finally, Jesus answered and said, "I am not sent but unto the lost sheep of the house of Israel." God's plan of salvation was to be extended first to the Jews and then to the Gentiles. His response was not enough to discourage this mother. Not only was her daughter suffering, but she as well because she could not bear to see her daughter vexed by evil spirits. She had counted the cost and was willing to go as far as necessary to get the results she knew only Jesus could provide. This woman worshipped him more and pleaded with Him to help her. The wholeness of her daughter meant more than anything. Jesus answered her again, it is not meet (right or fit) to take the childrens' bread and cast it to dogs. Many would have walked away, feeling that Jesus insulted them with name calling. However, this mother stated, "Truth, Lord: yet, the dogs eat the crumbs which fall from their master's table."

Bread is symbolic of the benefits the children of God enjoy as a result of establishing a relationship with Him. In the Bible days, people who did not have a relationship with God were referred to primarily as Gentiles, heathen or dogs. This was just the common terminology of that day. Jesus simply used the common terminology of the day to test the woman's faith. This woman acknowledged her position as undeserving since she had no legal right to the benefits of the kingdom. Kingdom benefits were for the children of the kingdom. She requested benefits for which she was not entitled to since she was not a partaker of the kingdom of God. She used the words of Jesus concerning dogs as grounds for further claim to healing for her daughter. Even dogs have rights to the crumbs that fall from their master's table. This mother claimed the scraps for her daughter. She was actually saying even the leftovers, if there be any, in the kingdom of God are of great value and on this premise I'll stand for my daughter's deliverance.

What boldness, what faith, what determination! Even Jesus marvelled at this. The Bible says, He answered and said unto her, "O woman, great is your faith: be it unto you even as you desire." Her daughter was made WHOLE from that very hour. What would have happened if the mother had given up prematurely?

Salvation carries with it great benefits. You are God's child and entitled to the childrens' bread (the blessings of God). You must develop the tenacity necessary to discipline yourself to get results at all costs. You must see yourself as God sees you and speak as He speaks. What do you have to lose? Words are powerful containers. They transfer inner images. The more you say what God has to say about you the more you build images within of the woman God created you to be. You are not hopeless, frail, worthless. **<u>YOU ARE A WOMAN OF GOD AND YOU ARE DESTINED FOR GREATNESS</u>**.

There is another case in scripture where Jesus met a Samaritan woman who had been married five times and upon her encounter with Jesus was living with a man. It is obvious for us to conclude, this woman's life was void of something. She was unfulfilled as a woman and I must venture to say she needed wholeness. Her answer could not be found in a mere man, sex or anything of the sort. (**John 4:4-30**) First of all, the Bible says Jesus must needs go through Samaria. I believe one of the reasons this statement carries so much importance is because Jesus knew there was a woman who desperately needed him in Samaria. This woman had to meet Him if her life was to be made whole. It's amazing that during this time in biblical history there was much prejudice against women. The Rabbis (ministers) were not allowed to converse with women in public or instruct them in the scriptures in public. Jews were not supposed to have anything to do with Samaritans. In spite of this, Jesus would not allow racial barriers, religious barriers or traditions of men to stop Him in His aim to transform this woman's life. Men highlight differences; God gets glory out of them.

Jesus meets the woman at a well named Jacob's well. She comes to draw water, and He asks her for water. She wonders how He can ask her for water when she is of a different race. Race has never been an issue with God nor a determining factor for one to receive the blessings of God. Jesus says to her, "If you knew the gift of God, and who it is that saith to thee, give me drink; you would have asked of him, and He would have given thee living water." She thinks Jesus is speaking of water in the literal sense, and says "Sir, thou hast nothing to draw with and the well is deep, from when then hast thou that living water? Art thou greater than our father Jacob, which gave us the well, and drank thereof himself, and his children and his cattle?" Jesus answered and said unto her, "Whosoever drinketh of this water shall thirst again. But whosoever drinketh of the water that I shall give him shall never thirst; but the water that I shall give him shall be in him a well of water springing up into everlasting life." The woman saith unto him, "Sir, give me this water that I thirst not, neither come hither to draw." She still focuses on water in the literal sense. Jesus is offering an eternal cure for her emptiness. He wants to effect a work on the inside that is lasting. In order to open her eyes and get to the root of the problem, He asks, "Go, call thy husband, and come here." The woman answered and said, "I have no husband." Jesus said unto her, "Thou hast well said, I have no husband: for thou hast had five husbands, and he whom thou now hast is not thy husband: in that saidst thou truly....". Now, with the bare facts staring her in the face, we approach the core of the situation. Jesus causes the woman to look inward and examine the situation. She was obviously missing something. The answer was not in all her dealings with these men. She lacked wholeness. She lacked self-worth and Jesus was there to make her a complete woman without physical or psychological tactics. This is why Jesus told her, "Whosoever drinketh of the water that I shall give him shall never thirst; but the water that I shall give him shall be in him a well of water springing up into everlasting life."

The problem was within and in order for her to be complete the transformation had to begin within. This could not begin until she turned her attention inward and recognized that she was void of something that only an encounter with the Almighty God could satisfy. Jesus exposed her very life before her in order that she could come to grips with what was actually happening in her life. Unless the woman was made whole, she would continue her search for fulfillment in all the wrong people and ways. No mortal man had her answer. Surely after five marriages and a present relationship, she had to conclude the same.

The woman becomes acquainted with Jesus as the Christ and tells an entire city, "Come see a man which told me all things that ever I did. Is not this the Christ?" What she was actually saying was that Jesus exposed her past, healed her emotional wounds and transformed her life. This experience gave her liberty (emancipation from bondage) and boldness to witness of His supernatural delivering power. Her aim was to lead others to someone greater who could do in them what he had done in her.

The Bible clearly reveals that Jesus cared about women. He took advantage of every opportunity to deal with impossibilities and defy traditions and the condemning nature of others. After being criticized on a number of occasions for being found in the company of sinners, Jesus said in **Mark 2:17**, "*...They that are **WHOLE** have no need of the physician, but they that are sick: I* *came not to call the righteous, but sinners to repentance."* Jesus knew that sickness was not restricted to the physical body but to the soul and spirit as well. He targeted in on the true source of the problem in order to bring deliverance to all who desired it.

Luke 8:2-3

And certain women, which had been healed of evil spirits and infirmities, Mary called Magdalene, out of whom went seven devils, and Joanna the wife of Chuza, Herod's steward, and Susanna, And many others, which ministered unto him of their substance.

The compassion Jesus extended to these women compelled them to follow Him and support Him eternally. This is a truth perhaps many men need to grasp. Genuine love and compassion will cause a woman to go above and beyond to to serve. Force and brutality breeds resistance and bitterness. God knows all about the man He created. It is His creation (mankind) who does not know Him as Creator, who experiences a sense of lost and is therefore void of fulfillment.

Before we end our search on wholeness in the lives of women and draw further conclusions, let's consider several more women:

In **John 8:1-11,** Jesus, tempted by the Pharisees, exemplifies great concern and compassion for a woman caught in adultery. According to the law, at that time, any woman caught in adultery was to be stoned to death. The Pharisees were not concerned about the woman found in adultery. They only desired to entrap Jesus into going against the law. However, Jesus puts them on the spot by saying, "He that is without sin among you, let him first cast a stone at her." Jesus stooped down as if He was writing on the ground as the crowd left one at a time. One of the most powerful truths is recorded in this statement. People in general make mistakes. People in general fail and people are not perfect. In **Romans 3:10**, the Bible says, *"There is none righteous, no not one."* So who is man that he should condemn another man?

No person has the right to conclude that one individual is worse than another lest he or she be exposed by God in light of their own dealings. So what if you make a mistake? You have been divorced one time, perhaps two? Big deal! God's mercy and His grace is far greater than the failures of men. A mistake does not mean the end of the world. What is done in spite of the mistake will determine future results. People may ridicule, but what does God say. Examine what Jesus says to this woman in spite of the accusation against her. "Where are those thine accusers? Hath no man condemned thee"? She said, "No man, Lord, and Jesus said unto her, "Neither do I condemn thee: go and sin no more." He says, if I being the Son of God, find you innocent, or guiltless; if I don't accuse you, if my forgiveness is sufficient, who is man that he could condemn you?

Jesus sets her on course for a new beginning because her past is not a factor any longer. Jesus did not condone the sin act, he simply forgave her, and dealt with the root of the situation thereby giving her the proper resources to discontinue her previous manner of living. He instructs her to refrain from her former lifestyle by saying,"Go and sin no more." He instructed her to allow the Word of God to govern how she would behave in days to come.

Your past is not a factor unless you make it one. What is important, is what you will do today.

Luke 7:37-39

And, behold, a woman in the city, which was a sinner, when she knew that Jesus sat at meat in the Pharisee's house, brought an alabaster box of ointment, and stood at his feet behind him weeping, and began to wash his feet with tears, and did wipe them with the hairs of her head, and kissed his feet, and anointed them with the ointment. Now when the Pharisee which had bidden him saw it, he spake within himself, saying, this man, if he were a prophet,

*would have known who and what manner of
woman this is that toucheth him: for she is a
sinner.*

Jesus was fully aware of this woman's condition spiritually,
emotionally and physically. What mattered to Him was the
fact that He came to heal the emotionally scarred, physically
handicapped and spiritually devastated life. Jesus saw the
internal wounds and it did not matter what the critics thought.
This is how Jesus handled the critics.

Luke 7:40-50

*And Jesus answering said unto him, Simon, I
have somewhat to say unto thee. And he saith,
Master, say on. There was a certain creditor
which had two debtors: the one owed five
hundred pence, and the other fifty. And when
they had nothing to pay, he frankly forgave
them both. Tell me, therefore, which of them
will love him most? Simon answered and
said, I suppose that he, to whom he forgave
most. And he said unto him, thou hast rightly
judged. And he turned to the woman, and
said unto Simon, seest thou this woman? I
entered into thine house, thou gavest me no
water for my feet: but she hath washed my
feet with tears, and wiped them with the hairs
of her head. Thou gavest me no kiss: but
this woman since the time I came in hath
not ceased to kiss my feet. My head with oil
thou didst not anoint: but this woman hath
anointed my feet with ointment. Wherefore I
say unto thee, her sins, which are many, are
forgiven; for she loved much: but to whom
little is forgiven, the same loveth little. And
he said unto her, thy sins are forgiven. And*

they that sat at meat with him began to say within themselves, who is this that forgiveth sins also? And he said to the woman, thy faith hath saved thee; go in peace.

This woman came to Jesus with respect and reverence. She acknowledged that she had failed in life. Her only hope was in her meeting someone greater than herself. People who knew of her past scorned her. Jesus saw the void in her life, the pain, and the desire to change. He honored her desire, healed the wounds, and positioned her for victory.

While Jesus was teaching in a church setting (synagogue) on the sabbath, (**Luke 13:10-13**) there was a woman which had a spirit (demonic spirit) of infirmity eighteen years and was bowed together and could in no wise lift up herself. Again, we must remember it was against religious tradition for Rabbis to converse with women in public, instruct them concerning spiritual things and touch them in any manner. Jesus defies tradition. When He saw her, He called her to Him and said unto her, "Woman thou are loosed from thine infirmity." And he laid his hands on her and immediately she was made straight (whole), and glorified God.

This woman needed physical wholeness and perhaps because of her physical ailment, she suffered emotionally as well. Jesus acknowledges that she is of the lineage of Abraham and has covenant rights. She is entitled to healing. She has a right to experience wholeness in every area of her life. He immediately called her to himself, laid his hands upon her and healed her of this condition.

Finally, we consider the story of Jairus' daughter and a woman who bled for twelve years.

Luke 8:41-55
And, behold, there came a man named Jairus, and he was a ruler of the synagogue: and he fell down at Jesus' feet, and besought him that

*he would come into his house: For he had
one only daughter, about twelve years of age,
and she lay a dying. But as he went the people
thronged him. And a woman having an issue
of blood twelve years, which had spent all
her living upon physicians, neither could be
healed of any, came behind him, and touched
the border of his garment: and immediately
her issue of blood stanched (dried up). And
Jesus said, Who touched me? When all
denied, Peter and they that were with him said,
Master, the multitude throng thee and press
thee, and sayest thou, Who touched me? And
Jesus said, somebody hath touched me: for
I perceive that virtue is gone out of me. And
when the woman saw that she was not hid, she
came trembling, and falling down before him,
she declared unto him before all the people
for what cause she had touched him, and how
she was healed immediately. And he said
unto her, Daughter, be of good comfort: thy
faith hath made thee **WHOLE**; go in peace.
While he yet spake, there cometh one from
the ruler of the synagogue's house, saying to
him, Thy daughter is dead; trouble not the
Master. But when Jesus heard it, he answered
him, saying, Fear not: believe only, and she
shall be made whole. And when he came into
the house, he suffered no man to go in, save
Peter, and James, and John, and the father
and the mother of the maiden. And all wept,
and bewailed her: but he said, Weep not; she
is not dead, but sleepeth. And they laughed
him to scorn, knowing that she was dead. And
he put them all out, and took her by the hand,*

*and called saying, Maid, arise. And her spirit
came again, and she arose straightway: and
he commanded to give her meat.*

The woman who had been bleeding for twelve years had spent all that she had going from physician to physician. In **Mark 5:26**, the Bible says she got worse. One day she heard Jesus was in town. This was her opportunity for change. This was her opportunity for a miracle. Even though she knew it was against Jewish law for her to be out in her condition (bleeding) and that she could be killed if this was known, she dared to take a risk. She chose to risk her life in order to gain life; in order to be made whole. I am sure she felt that if she don't go, she would soon die, and there was nothing to lose and much to gain. Even though the situation dictated defeat, she did not accept defeat. She had faith to believe that even where the doctors failed, Jesus had enough power in His very clothes to transform her condition, and transform He did.

Jesus took time with this woman. He will take time with you if you are willing to take a risk. He went on in spite of the negative news concerning Jairus' daughter and performed another miracle. Do you see the key? No matter what the odds are against you, there is someone greater than the odds who cares about you.

The following scriptures reveal the perfect will of God for all His children and the power of His spoken word:

Matthew 8:16-17
*When the even was come, they brought unto
him many that were possessed with devils:
and he cast out the spirits with his word,
and healed all that were sick: that it might
be fulfilled which was spoken by Esaias the
prophet, saying, Himself took our infirmities,
and bare our sicknesses.*

Acts 10:38
*How God anointed Jesus of Nazareth with
the Holy Ghost and with power: who went*

about doing good, and healing all that were
oppressed of the devil; for God was with him.

In each situation we notice that it is the will of God for these women to be whole women. God's will for you today is that you become a complete woman in every area of your life. If it was God's will for these women to continue the course they were taking, Jesus would not have ministered to them immediately providing the relief they so desperately longed for. It is not God's will for your life to be a wreck, or for you to be emotionally distraught or physically discomforted.

We also see that it took a close up encounter with Jesus before the wholeness of every woman was realized. These women suffered until they became acquainted with Jesus, and you must become acquainted with him first if your wholeness, your deliverance and your healing will be realized. Each woman had to recognize that she had a problem that was greater than herself.

They acquired the knowledge necessary for change and prevailed against the odds to receive the desired results.

Wholeness will always begin with a relationship with Jesus. After receiving Him as Lord and Savior, which simply means you no longer desire to live by the world's standards, but you purpose to live pleasing before God. This is accomplished by obedience to the principles He has revealed before you in His Word, (the Bible).

You no longer need to make excuses for the past. Simply begin to live a one day at a time looking to God for daily instruction. Don't settle for less than God's best. God has ordained that you possess the capacity to enjoy life as you walk complete in HIM, lacking no good thing.

Proverbs 3:1-6

My son, forget not my law; but let thine
heart keep my commandments: For length
of days, and long life, and peace, shall they
add to thee. Let not mercy and truth forsake

83

thee: bind them about thy neck; write them upon the table of thine heart: So shalt thou find favour and good understanding in the sight of God and man. Trust in the Lord with all thine heart; and lean not unto thine own understanding. In all thy ways acknowledge him, and he shall direct thy paths.

Isaiah 55:8-11

For my thoughts are not your thoughts, neither are your ways my ways, saith the Lord. For as the heavens are higher than the earth, so are my ways higher than your ways, and my thoughts than your thoughts. For as the rain cometh down, and the snow from heaven, and returneth not thither, but watereth the earth, and maketh it bring forth and bud, that it may give seed to the sower, and bread to the eater: so shall my word be that goeth forth out of my mouth: it shall not return unto me void, but it shall accomplish that which I please, and it shall prosper in the thing whereto I sent it.

You have begun your journey to wholeness. I did not say your journey would be easy or challenge free, but it will be rewarding if you'll work at being the best "YOU", you can be. This is the time when you must demand growth of yourself. Wholeness will not come if you are determined to rehearse the shattering events of the past. It is important that you refrain from meditating on and discussing yesterday's mishaps. Refuse to be persuaded by others who are familiar with your past to rehearse it. If you are not bold enough to tell them "you are a new creature with a new beginning," perhaps you should separate yourself from their company until that boldness comes. You do not have time to rehearse the events of the past. Forgive yourself and forgive others. Don't brood over hurts and offenses as this only triggers self-pity.

As long as we live on planet earth and interact with people, offenses will come, but we do not have to react to the offense. Beginning today you must allow your heart and mind to be governed by God's Word. You will have the ability to handle any and everything as you develop in prayer. Prayer is simply talking to God and allowing God to talk to you. It is this communication with the Father that will build a reinforcement in you that enables you to overcome the weakness in the flesh and soul, and provide you with a greater sensitivity to the Spirit of God.

Colossians 3:8-17

But now ye also put off all these; anger, wrath, malice, blasphemy, filthy communication out of your mouth. Lie not one to another, seeing that ye have put off the old man with his deeds; and have put on the new man, which is renewed in knowledge after the image of him that created him: where there is neither Greek nor Jew, circumcision nor uncircumcision, Barbarian, Scythian, bond nor free: but Christ is all, and in all. Put on therefore, as the elect of God, holy and beloved, bowels of mercies, kindness, humbleness of mind, meekness, longsuffering; forbearing one another, and forgiving one another, if any man have a quarrel against any: even as Christ forgave you, so also do ye. And above all these things put on charity, which is the bond of perfectness. And let the peace of God rule in your hearts, to the which also ye are called in one body; and be ye thankful. Let the Word of Christ dwell in you richly in all wisdom; teaching and admonishing one another in Psalm and hymns and spiritual songs, singing with grace in your hearts to the Lord. And whatsoever ye do in word or deed, do all in

the name of the Lord Jesus, giving thanks to
God and the Father by him.

Perhaps it seems that God requires a lot of us. My response is, He requires no more than He is willing to give for us. This was proved when He gave His best. **HE GAVE ALL. HE GAVE HIS SON. ACTUALLY, HE GAVE HIMSELF.**

Daily you must continue to look into your physical mirror after looking into the mirror of God's word and say what God says about you. Spend quiet time talking to the Lord daily and practice improving yourself. Even while working on the inside with the assistance of the Holy Spirit, remember God wants you to experience wholeness in all areas. Allow Him to direct you as you improve your outward appearance as well. Perhaps you have neglected areas you once took pride in. For example, getting a manicure and pedicure. You might want to lose weight. Maybe you would like a new hairstyle. Change is a choice. Make the decision to reward yourself. Buy a bottle of perfume, treat yourself to dinner and understand this clearly: the acquisition of things or the absence of things have nothing to do with your self-worth or value as a woman. Jesus said in **Mark 12:15,** *"...beware of covetousness: for a man's life consisteth not in the abundance of the things which he possesseth."* A life rich in God and inner peace in abundance is of far greater value than the wealth of this world. Materialistic things do not dictate your position in God. **<u>YOU ARE GOD'S WOMAN</u>. YOU DESERVE THE BEST AND YOU WILL NEVER HAVE A NEED FOR WHICH HE IS NOT THE TOTAL AND ABSOLUTE SUPPLY.**

CHAPTER FIVE

RECOVERY IN INTIMACY

This chapter is written primarily for those who have been victims of rape, molestation, incest, or forced sex in any manner. Often, as a result of this violation and the brutality and vulgarity associated with it, many women find it difficult to experience fulfillment in intimacy. You can recover from the effects of sex violations and enjoy a marital relationship filled with the rewards of genuine intimacy if you choose to. I speak exclusively on this topic in relationship confined to the institution of "holy matrimony."

As with any area let's look at this topic from God's perspective. If we understand God's purpose for ordaining lovemaking, we can better understand the recovery process. God's word is the standard by which we live and His Word, once we commit to it, governs every area of life. God does not view lovemaking as mere "sex." He highly ordained lovemaking as a sacred act before Him which is tied to a significant spiritual reference. The act of lovemaking transcends emotions and physical attraction. As with every area of a Christian's life, lovemaking should bring honor and glory to God.

Sex as the world knows it has been everything but holy as God designed it to be. The devil has purposely influenced men and women to disregard the commandment of God and contaminate a most sacred act endorsed by God. It is no longer regarded as an expression of love between a man and woman in the confines of marriage. It is in most instances, casual, meaningless, perverted and self-gratifying at the expense of others. Sex, as the world looks upon it, happens among people who have no knowledge of each other, no relationship just "**IF IT FEELS GOOD, DO IT.**"

Fornication is the act of engaging in sex before marriage. Let's see how seriously God views this indulgence.

I Thessalonians 4:3

For this is the will of God, even your sanctification, that ye should abstain from fornication:...

I Corinthians 6:13b-20

...Now the body is not for fornication, but for the Lord; and the Lord for the body. And God hath both raised up the Lord, and will also raise up us by his own power. Know ye not that your bodies are the members of Christ? Shall I then take the members of Christ, and make them the members of a harlot? GOD FORBID. What? Know ye not that he which is joined to an harlot is one body? For two, saith he, shall be one flesh. But he that is joined unto the Lord is one spirit. Flee fornication. Every sin that a man doeth is without the body; but he that committeth fornication sinneth against his own body. What? Know ye not that your body is the temple of the Holy Ghost which is in you, which ye have of God, and ye are not your own? For ye are bought with a price: therefore glorify God in your body, and in your spirit, which are God's.

I Corinthians 5:11

But now I have written unto you not to keep company, if any man that is called a brother be a fornicator, or covetous, or an idolater, or a railer, or a drunkard, or an extortioner; with such an one no not to eat.

Revelation 21:8

But the fearful, and unbelieving, and the abominable, and murderers, and whoremongers, and sorcerers, and idolaters,

and all liars, shall have their part in the lake
which burneth with fire and brimstone: which
is the second death.

The Bible distinctively expresses that everything God created is good. God observed Adam and declared, "It is not good that man should be alone." He skillfully handcrafted someone suitable and adaptable to Adam. God fashioned woman and brought her to man. The institution of marriage was first ordered by God. God gave to Adam and Eve, as He has to every male and female, a precious gift. This gift is virginity. This virgin state is priceless and designed to remain until the entrance into the bonds of "holy matrimony."

Genesis 2:24-25
Therefore shall a man leave his father and his
mother, and shall cleave unto his wife: and
they shall be one flesh. And they were both
*naked, the man and **HIS WIFE**, and were not*
ashamed.

Within the woman's body God fashioned a fold of mucous membrane partly closing the opening of the vagina. This membrane is called the "hymen." When a man and "HIS WIFE" engage in their first encounter of lovemaking, this membrane in the woman is broken. Once it is broken it bleeds. Because of the intimate nature of the man and "HIS WIFE", the blood must touch the male partner. God has designed this as the procedure by which the two become one.

In His infinite wisdom, God knew Adam and Eve would sin and fall from the holy state He fashioned them in originally. Only the shedding of innocent blood would reconcile man and woman back to God after sin entered the earth. God designed lovemaking as the entrance into a holy relationship with a blood covenant. Symbolically, it portrays the entrance into the family of God by virtue of a blood covenant initiated when Jesus Christ shed His blood for mankind. Acceptance of Jesus Christ causes an individual to enter into a blood covenant agreement with Almighty God.

Colossians 1:14
In whom we have redemption through his blood, even the forgiveness of sins:...

The institution of marriage is ordained as the only place such a sacred and intimate encounter as lovemaking should take place. Violation of this holy act is an outright violation against God.

As a result of violating God's order, the consequences are shocking. The joy of childbearing and raising a family has little or no value. Infants are aborted by the thousands. Relationships are polluted by unfaithfulness. Divorce statistics continue to rise. AIDs and so many other terminal illnesses are destroying lives by the millions. The shame and guilt associated with loose living, in essence, disobedience, is devastating.

Men and women are driven by the lust of their flesh not the mandate of God. God ordained lovemaking as more than just an enjoyable experience as the world has defined it. God endorsed a higher mandate. He endorsed the establishment of a covenant relationship.

If your virginity was taken from you, or, if you compromised before marriage, you can still enter into this God ordained covenant spiritually. As we have learned in the prior chapters, the soul must be renewed. We must take on God's perspective and allow His perspective to influence our attitude and thinking concerning intimacy. We must forgive those who violated us if our virginity was taken, and if we compromised before marriage we must forgive ourselves. We must release the thoughts, offenders, memories, attitudes, and hurts with the words of our mouth. Praying the following prayer with confidence in the power of God to heal and restore is essential to recovery:

Father, in Jesus name, as an act of my will, I choose to forgive those who robbed me of the gift of virginity. I release them now and commit them to you. You said if I did not forgive neither would I be forgiven. I need your forgiveness and therefore I forgive those who offended me. Heal the hurt and restore the joy of my covenant relationship with You. Father, I receive your forgiveness and declare with the words of my mouth, I AM FREE FROM THE TORMENTING EFFECTS OF ANY FORM OF SEX VIOLATION WHETHER FORCED OR BY MY OWN COMPROMISE. I commit my body to you afresh and will bring glory to you in my spirit, my soul and my body from this day forward. I will bring my body and my desires under control. Holy Spirit I appreciate You for keeping me, strengthening me and empowering me as I obey God's Word. I am now free to enjoy intimacy in marriage as never before. This is my covenant right. In Jesus Name, Amen!

Now, you are free to walk in wholeness. Remember, harboring the frustrations and hurts of the past in the heart will forever hinder intimate fulfillment in your marriage presently or should you decide to marry, in the days to come.

God can give you a mate who will love you as Christ loves the Church and bless your times of intimacy as never before. Sex outside of marriage is an abomination before God and brings certain consequences. God is present in the sanctity of marriage. You will be able to enjoy freedom in the area of intimacy through His healing power. If your spiritual relationship is pure and undefiled, your intimate relationship can be pure and undefiled.

Hebrews 13:4

Marriage is honourable in all, and the bed undefiled: but whoremongers and adulterers God will judge.

Proverbs 5:18-19

Let thy fountain be blessed: and rejoice with the wife of thy youth. Let her be as the loving hind and pleasant roe; let her breasts satisfy thee at all times; and be thou ravished always with her love.

God's Word is the cleansing agent. God explains in His Word that our bodies represent His body. Let me ask a question. Can you allow a man to cheapen what God has declared holy and set apart? God says you are holy. The tormenting effects of disobedience before marriage will be uprooted in time. Give yourself time to heal and refuse to entertain or rehearse the haunting memories.

This is an example of how the devil made attempts to torment me. When I married at age eighteen, I remember the man I married holding me down and forcibly gratifying himself. I hated him and I hated the sex act. I could see in my mind my father molesting me and my neighbor violating me. Sex was not beautiful. It was ugly. It was dirty. It was disgusting. I recognize so clearly now the protective hand of God warning us not to engage in sex before marriage. He knew of the pain and tormenting memories it would cause in a true marital relationship.

Many of you are in marriages where you lack fulfillment. The memories of the past always seem to haunt you at those times when your mate desires you intimately. You can experience wholeness once again even as I have. I have already explained how to release the hurts of the past; even as you begin to see yourself as God sees you and say what God says about you. You must see intimacy as ministry. Spend quality time fellowshipping with God and ministering to Him. He will teach you how to minister to your mate. Tenderness and excitement will come as you understand that you and your mate are in covenant with each other and together the two of you, now one before God, are in covenant with God.

You can nurture and build your relationship with your husband as you are open and honest with him. Remember we saw that

Adam and Eve were both naked and they were not ashamed. There is more to this than just the fact that they were physically naked. The true emphasis is on the fact that they were covered by the **GLORY OF GOD** and experienced genuine liberty in God. They experienced divine protection. Their inner most feelings were exposed, their innocence and their desire was not to abuse or take advantage of each other. Their desire was to explore the needs of one another and satisfy those needs unselfishly. This can only be experienced if you have known the love of God. Only God's love can give unselfishly and unconditionally.

Woman of God, you are clean before God. Stand in your position as the beautiful creature God made you to be. You are destined for GREATNESS in all areas of your life, even in the most intimate times with your mate.

John 15:3-7

Now ye are clean through the word which I have spoken unto you. Abide in me, and I in you. As the branch cannot bear fruit of itself, except it abide in the vine; no more can ye, except ye abide in me. I am the vine, ye are the branches: he that abideth in me, and I in him, the same bringeth forth much fruit: for without me ye can do nothing. If a man abide not in me, he is cast forth as a branch, and is withered; and men gather them, and cast them into the fire, and they are burned. If ye abide in me, and my words abide in you, ye shall ask what ye will, and it shall be done unto you.

I Corinthians 7:5

Defraud ye not one the other, except it be with consent for a time, that ye may give yourselves to fasting and prayer; and come together again, that satan tempt you not for your incontinency.

God is so wise and protective. In **I Corinthians 7:5**, He explains that there are times in marriage when the husband or wife may desire to spend time fasting and praying. It is during these times, based upon mutual consent, that the husband and wife refrain from intimacy in order that they seek the Lord in a more consecrated way. He tells them after the agreed upon interval to come together and lovingly minister to one another in order that satan cannot interfere, and tempt them into unfaithfulness.

To the single women who still possess God's gift of virginity, if you'll adhere to God's Word the devil will never use tormenting tactics in the realm of your mind such as comparing your future husband with past relationships. If you'll keep yourselves for your GOD-ORDAINED HUSBAND there will be no one the devil can use to compare him to. He will be the first (as God intended) and only. It is not your job to search for a husband. God will cause your paths to cross supernaturally. Sure, you'll make the choice but God does the drawing.

If you are single but not a virgin, God can do His greatest work in you. He will preserve you by the power of the Holy Spirit and teach you how to control those God given desires until marriage. The desires you have are not evil but they are reserved.

Proverbs 18:22
Whoso findeth a wife findeth a good thing, and obtaineth favour of the Lord.

Women don't violate God's order being ruled by your emotions and looking for a man. Stay positioned before God. He will cause YOUR MATE to find you. I experienced devastating consequences as a result of my eagerness to marry before the appointed time. There is such a thing as proper timing. God has ordained a proper time for all things. Being anxious can only lead to disappointment.

Ecclesiastes 3:1
To every thing there is a season, and a time to every purpose under the heaven:...

Galatians 4:4-5

But when the fulness of the time was come,
God sent forth his Son, made of a woman,
made under the law, To redeem them that
were under the law, that we might receive the
adoption of sons.

You don't have to make the same mistakes as others. It is better to enjoy the blessings of God than the consequences that lack of patience can bring.

Whether you were divorced, widowed, violated by force or compromise, God's will is that you recover and experience His glory and freedom in marital intimacy. This process of recovery will not happen overnight, but it will happen. All that I have shared is factual. You are not beyond the point of recovery. When I examine my life and all that God has done, I must affirm--"**IF YOU CAN BELIEVE, NOTHING SHALL BE IMPOSSIBLE TO YOU.**" God supernaturally healed me internally, and when I say my life was a nightmare, this statement is by no means to be taken lightly. This book cannot contain some of the horrors I could share with you in explicit detail. I am proof that God transforms, heals, delivers and restores. There is no one I can compare my mate to today. He surpasses all others. He cherishes me, but more importantly "HE LOVES ME AS CHRIST LOVES THE CHURCH"--completely, freely, unconditionally and honestly. God can and will do the same for YOU. Don't settle for failure. Remember, failure is not automatic. It requires your permission. God can do for you and in you what you are willing to allow Him to.

Recovery is a process that is available to you. Receive it and reap the benefits of wholeness in every area of your life.

Luke 4:18-19

The Spirit of the Lord is upon me, because
he hath anointed me to preach the gospel
to the poor; he hath sent me to heal the

brokenhearted, to preach deliverance to the captives, and recovering of sight to the blind, to set at liberty them that are bruised, to preach the acceptable year of the Lord.

CHAPTER SIX

CONCLUSION
(WOMAN BE WHOLE)

It is apparent that the devil can manipulate circumstances to rob you of the blessings of God. It is also true that you decide how you will respond to the circumstances of life. People may come against you and do some negative things to harm you, however, you will ultimately decide what the outcome will be. Situations may require responses, but you do not have to react adversely. You are in control and must take charge of your life. What's in your heart and spoken out of YOUR mouth will create life or death. Even though you submit to God and commit to His Word, you will not be immune to the challenges of life. However, you will overcome every challenge with the tools you have been given in this book.

The Bible speaks of a situation concerning Lazarus (**John 11:1-44**) that shook me in a profound manner. Jesus received word that a friend whom He loved was sick. When He arrived in Bethany, his friend had been dead for four days. Jesus never allowed the report of others to dictate His actions. He went to the place where His friend was buried and told those with Him to move the stone concealing the grave. He then cried, "Lazarus come forth." He that was dead came forth, bound hand and foot with grave clothes and his face was bound about with a napkin. Jesus saith unto them, "Loose him and let Him go."

In this situation God reveals how an individual can be alive physically and spiritually and still be bound by the odor of death (grave clothes-bondage). To be bound means to be tormented, limited, held captive, restricted. Lazarus was alive but I am sure being bound with grave clothes was tormenting and uncomfortable to say the least. He had been acquainted with Jesus before the physical death. He was acquainted with Jesus after being resurrected but bondage still existed. He had no mobility and no freedom to enjoy life. He was held hostage. It took the Word of God, spoken by the mouth of Jesus, and the assistance of others to give him the liberty needed to enjoy resurrected life.

Those who receive Jesus as Lord and Savior experience resurrection (new life). Often, even after experiencing a relationship with Jesus, one can still be in bondage. This is where I was. It took the power of God (the Holy Spirit), His Word, and the assistance of others to bring freedom. I had to be loosed from the effects of grave clothes. Today I am free to enjoy resurrected life.

As I consider all that has been shared in this book, I realize there are women who feel so badly about themselves that they will not change their circumstances. The odor of death is holding them captive. There are women who are being abused day after day. Many stay in abusive situations only to allow torment and fear to continue. In their minds they literally justify that torture is what they deserve. They are convinced this is their lot in life. To these women, I SAY, you have the Word of God, the Holy Spirit and the assistance of others available to you, but the choice is yours. If you will begin to believe about yourself what God believes about you, your will find a <u>WHOLE</u> new fullness in life.

There are people all over the world who believe they are poor because they are supposed to be poor (poverty mentality). At the same time, there are people who are unsuccessful because they believe they are supposed to be unsuccessful. Let's set the record straight. **<u>GOD IS NOT A CHILD ABUSER.</u>** He wants absolutely nothing but the best for His children. Being His child does not exempt you from challenges. There is a thief (the devil) who will always attempt to interfere with you experiencing God's best.

Many use the excuse, "Well if God really wants it to be, it will be." This is not a true statement. God wants everyone to be holy, but that does not mean everyone will be holy. God gave

Jesus in order that everyone could experience salvation. You and I know not everyone will be saved and enjoy everlasting life. The woman who sets the course in her life for CHANGE will rise above the norm. This woman will rise up above the problem. She will rise above the circumstance and experience the joy of new life as her reward.

There is one thing people who are successful possess that unsuccessful people don't have. Successful people never allow a sour deal to dictate the result of future endeavors or rob them of their goals, dreams, and determination. Many people with a defeated attitude, no hope, no vision for life and poor perception of themselves, life and others, make very few attempts, if any, to really stretch themselves. As we discussed, the confidence level of an individual will determine his or her level of success.

Being a whole person does not mean you will never make a mistake; neither does it mean challenges won't frustrate you periodically. Being a whole person says you are ready to handle any and all challenges. You are no longer tormented by the discomfort of grave clothes because the stone of shame, guilt, and so much more has been rolled away. If you make a mistake you repent and learn from the mistake how to handle similar situations for the future. A mistake not learned from will be repeated. There must be repentance when mistakes are made and a positive course of action taken to alleviate repeating the same mistake.

Battles only surround the birth of a miracle and with this concept you'll overcome every obstacle with a winning attitude.

You are God's "crowning glory" and He has placed you in a position of dominion. You were created by God to be like God. Take back that "Godly Image" and confidence the devil stole. Be the overcomer God predestined you to be. Dare to make the difference.

Living in the past only robs you of the time required to fulfill God's best in you **TODAY**. Enjoy the dimension of wholeness revealed in God's Word and allow Him to continue to fashion you into the **BEST INDIVIDUAL YOU CAN BE IN HIM**. You are God's woman and certainly, you are destined for greatness. To "be" is a state of being. Woman you are WHOLE! Live a life filled with the Word of God and total dependance on His Spirit. Always operate in the law of forgiveness and trust God to elevate you from one dimension to another. I have attempted to flood you with God's Word. Now, you must continue to daily declare who you are in God as you develop your relationship with Him. A powerful truth about relationship is, the one you spend the most time with and allow to influence you the most is the one you become conformed to. The more time you spend with our Heavenly Father, the more your life will be conformed to His standard of living. This is "ZOE" life (life in the highest form). Life on this plateau with the Master will never rehearse the offenses of the past. Life on this plateau builds on the expectations of the future. **WOMAN BE WHOLE**.

For Tape and Book Catalog write to:

Time of Celebration Ministries Church
C/O Jacqueline T. Flowers
P. O. Box 671522
Houston, Texas 77267-1522

Made in the USA
Monee, IL
22 September 2023

43060889R00069